The Collected Stories of
Ingrid Dickson

RED SKY NIGHTS

Thirty baffling World War II stories
as witnessed by a young girl growing up
in Berlin, Germany

© 2019 Red Sky Nights The Collected Stories of Ingrid Dickson
Published posthumously by Echoludo

Acknowledgments

Thanks to Gray La Fond, Dr. Kelly Lange, Dr. Steve La Fond, the children and relatives of Ingrid Dickson and for all those friends and family, who eagerly, yet patiently, waited for Ingrid's stories to be brought to life in print, digital and audio formats.

Copyright©2019
Red Sky Nights: The Collected Stories of Ingrid Dickson

ISBN-13: 978-1-7334318-1-1

Library of Congress Registration Number TXu 2-160-719

Published in 2019 by Echoludo

All rights reserved. No part of this book, e-book or audiobook may be reproduced or transmitted in any form or by any means, electronic or mechanical, including photocopying, recording, or by any information storage and retrieval system, without the publisher's written permission.

Transcription and text edited by Gray La Fond and Dr. Kelly Lange
Audio edited by Echoludo
Cover designed by Echoludo

www.echoludo.com

In loving memory of Ingrid Dickson

(December 4, 1936 - March 8, 2019)

This book is dedicated to a life fully lived without regrets.
Ingrid danced through life with a spirit of open-minded
curiosity and a soul full of creative joy.

About the Author

Ingrid Dickson was born in 1936 to German parents. Ingrid's mother was raised in a circus family led by Ingrid's grandfather, who was the trapeze "flier." She and her sister, Ingrid's aunt, were trained to perform in a side-show. Together, they created a sister-act that included singing, dancing, and acrobatic horses. When Ingrid's mother married, she gave up performance. However, Ingrid's aunt went on to establish her career as a song and dance performer, as noted in some of the stories.

When the war began, due to his technical expertise, Ingrid's father was forced to work as an engineer for the Nazi Party under the threat of death to him and his entire family. Not much is known about his work. However, Ingrid described memories of riding with him in large cavalcades of decorated limousines, and on occasion, visiting the beach with Hitler. After the war, Ingrid's father was offered professional asylum by the United States and the USSR. He refused both and stayed in Germany making small, hand-held radios for a living.

Under the infamous, harrowing circumstances of WWII, despite Ingrid's father's high-ranking position, his own family got entangled in life-threatening situations often with no hope to be seen. Ingrid's stories describe how her mother chose to act with an indomitable spirit of hope, courage and creativity to find a way through.

Publisher's Note to the Reader

RED SKY NIGHTS The Collected Stories of Ingrid Dickson has been published by Echoludo in unabridged audio, digital and print editions. All formats match word-for-word. The audiobook is composed of original recordings during which Ingrid told all of her own stories without a script.

The editors' intention during the project has always been to remain loyal to Ingrid's memories and to preserve her exact words. However, Ingrid's first language is German, and, although she speaks English, sometimes her English words fall into a more German grammatical structure so the reader may notice some oddities throughout the audio and text. The editors chose to leave some stories as is so that Ingrid's intrinsic character would not be lost by deletion or correction. As a reader and listener, please take this point into account as a small price to pay for her otherwise perfectly intriguing storytelling style

Ingrid is and was a true storyteller, down to her very bones. She had an uncanny reputation for being able to talk the paint off the walls. And when she started telling a story, it was difficult for anyone to step away because she always had another, "Oh! And did I tell you about the time...?"

Many people had heard Ingrid tell some of her baffling World War II stories in person and had encouraged her to write them down. However, Ingrid wasn't a writer and kept a busy, ink-filled calendar of theater, symphony and volunteer activities.

I met Ingrid Dickson in 2010 when, as luck would have it, I moved into the apartment next door to her. We shared a love for everything creative and despite our 30-year age difference quickly became friends, attending the symphony, theater, writing groups, and photography sessions together.

One evening, at our apartment building, Ingrid told me her war story called "Throwing Bread at Trains." That evening stretched into the early morning hours in story after story. I listened with untiring patience fueled by fascination. I was particularly inspired by the uncanny acts of Ingrid's mother. To me, she represented a woman of unique courage, who was thrown into war conditions with two young children, and yet was able to see past the horror of the situations, to take creative actions, and to make her way through when no one else saw hope or a way out.

That's when I realized the value of these stories and Ingrid's desire to share them so people can learn from her experience. It struck me that if I didn't write them down, it was possible Ingrid's stories might not ever be heard so we signed a contract together to publish her book.

During a year's worth of Friday afternoons, I recorded Ingrid telling her stories in the quiet privacy of my office. Due to the closeness of our relationship, I believe Ingrid's audiobook gives listeners a uniquely intimate feeling of sharing memories with a trusted friend.

Originally, I had intended to simply transcribe the audio and publish the book. However, when the audio was transcribed, the sentences appeared tangled and hard to read. In fact, the first editor we approached said the project was impossible and would never work. Since both the audio and the transcript needed intensive editing and restructuring, I decided to dig in further and publish the audio, digital and print book matching word-for-word.

At this point in our process, Ingrid's health started to decline, and I took on the responsibilities of her caregiving as well. Although this stretched out our process, we were both motivated to finish the book.

Fortunately, the project was blessed by a bright, young editor named Gray La Fond. We met Gray when Ingrid was transferred to a nursing home. Gray happened to be the child of Ingrid's primary care doctor and had crossed our path out of pure coincidence. Gray showed a passion for WWII, compassion for Ingrid's creative life, and an interest in the project. Together Gray and I took on the daunting process of transcription, text restructuring and audio editing using all the original recordings.

The process chugged along slowly for two years through four rounds of text and audio editing. Gray and I met at Ingrid's nursing home weekly and sat beside her reading each story word-for-word. Sadly, near the end of our editing, Ingrid's ability to speak was reduced to yes or no answers.

This audio, digital, and print book represents a celebration of Ingrid Dickson's unique moments lived during a time of extreme global war and chaos. Her life experiences are memorialized here for all of us through her words.

RED SKY NIGHTS

Table of Contents

CHAPTER 1
    WHY? 14
CHAPTER 2
    DR. PILLERMAN 16
CHAPTER 3
    CHILDREN LOVE A PARADE 22
CHAPTER 4
    MURDER AT THE STREETCAR STOP 26
CHAPTER 5
    FAMILY ABDUCTED 30
CHAPTER 6
    FIRE IN THE BASEMENT 34
CHAPTER 7
    DANGEROUS MISTAKEN IDENTITY 38
CHAPTER 8
    WAITING IN LINE FOR BREAD 44
CHAPTER 9
    SCHOOL KIDS ON THE FRONT 50
CHAPTER 10
    GRANDMOTHER'S NEIGHBORHOOD 54
CHAPTER 11
    THE BUNKER 58
CHAPTER 12
    RED SKY NIGHTS 64
CHAPTER 13
    HERR TÜCHLER'S QUIET ESCAPE 68
CHAPTER 14
    RUNAWAYS 74
CHAPTER 15
    THROWING BREAD AT TRAINS 78

PHOTOGRAPHS 86

CHAPTER 16
THE MILK CAN 92

CHAPTER 17
YOU ARE MY SUNSHINE 98

CHAPTER 18
TEN DAYS IN THE LINE OF FIRE 104

CHAPTER 19
THE BRIDGE OVER THE RIVER ELBE 108

CHAPTER 20
CLIMBING LIKE A MONKEY 112

CHAPTER 21
THE RUSSIANS ARRIVE 116

CHAPTER 22
CAPTURED BY THE RUSSIANS 122

CHAPTER 23
JUMPING OVER THE RIVER FOR BREAD 128

CHAPTER 24
COMRADES IN VICTORY 134

CHAPTER 25
ESCAPE ON A PAINTED HORSE 138

CHAPTER 26
MAKING FLAGS OVERNIGHT 146

CHAPTER 27
CHIPMUNKING... 156

CHAPTER 28
ALL GREEN.. 162

CHAPTER 29
POTATO SHOES.. 170

CHAPTER 30
HERR TÜCHLER RETURNS.............................. 176

CHAPTER 1

WHY?

The purpose of the stories is to warn the public of brainwash, including the children.

They hear these stories and they can say, "I don't think this is good. I don't want that."

A person like Hitler, or big kings, they have a great need to be in power. They don't want nobody to object to anything they say or think. You're not supposed to ask. You're not supposed to question anything. They want to be obeyed; that's where they feel the power. And people bow to them.

And so, little by little, they become worse and worse, and when they didn't get enough power, then they do it even harsher. This repeats as this kind of "lifestyle" keeps developing, which ended with concentration camps. It happened then and it can happen again.

As children, things happen and it looks very strange to you—you've never seen this—you ask,

"What's the matter?" or "Why is this?"

But parents had to tell the child to hush up for survival reasons, but you still have the questions, unanswered, inside.

I did because when I see this horror, I think about how dangerous it is, how these few people do enough to upset everybody. How we ruin things.

We have to learn to love. Don't encourage any kind of war. If you have grievances, yes, you should talk about it, but don't get physical. Don't call them names. Don't push them around. Don't give them a hard time. Leave them alone and give them their peace, animal and people.

Teach peace and love. It's so common as a cliché now, but peace and love. Practice it. Practice it. In your family, in your school, your neighborhood, wherever you are.

Think about these things. And that is just something people really should think about.

CHAPTER 2

DR. PILLERMAN

I must have been four, something like that. My father often gave a little meeting, arranged in our apartment. My mother was there, too, but she would not be in the room where the meeting is happening. She'd prepare coffee cake and all the dishes, and make it nice for guests. They had all the lights on. She had a big, round table in the center and a tablecloth down to the floor. It was prepared very nice. This party was for the evening. They were all SS officers.

And I had this little baby doll which was my favorite. And I had learned a little poem from somebody and I was so proud of knowing this little poem. And say, "Lieber Doktor Pillermann, see der mal mein Püppchen an," which means "My dear Doctor 'Pill-Man,' look at my little doll." Like the doctor for dolls. "Something's wrong with her." Just very short little poem. So we rehearsed it before anybody came. My mother had me climb under the table where the tablecloth reached the floor. And all the chairs were set all the way around.

So she said, "You go under there, with your doll, but you don't make a sound. Don't touch nobody because they're going to come in and they're all going to sit and serve cake and the whipped cream, and the da, da da da, da." This is a German custom: when you have guests, you serve cake and coffee.

"Don't let them know you're there. And then I will say, 'My little daughter has learned a poem and she would like to demonstrate that poem for you.'" She will say, "You can do it now," and I will hear that and then I start. "Until then, you sit there. You're quiet. Don't touch nobody."

So, I remember to this day all the boots. You know how they used to have boots. They all sit around, and there were all these boots around in a circle, and I'm sitting in the middle with my doll.

Ha, he he he! Isn't that ridiculous? Like my performance in the theater is coming up and I have a little stage fright.

So I did everything. I sit very quiet, didn't say nothing, nothing, nothing. I have my doll, and I wait until I hear my mother give the cue.

So, they're talking and they're having lots of conversations. They were all SS officers. There were two of them who were young and they were new at it. And one of them, they ask him to tell some story that bothered him. And I heard the story. You know, it's amazing that I remember.

And he said that a bunch of Jews were put outdoors somewhere. And they're all standing together, at least twenty-two or so, I remember that. The Jewish people were all kinds, older and any ages. And then there were other SS guys with rifles on the sides. This was a test for him to be accepted for some special mission.

He said, "They gave me a rifle."

He was ordered, "'You go up there in front of them, and you kill them. You shoot them all. And when you did that successfully, you pass the test."

Not so good job, obviously.

He was young, but not a child. He was maybe twenty-some. I remember him, dishwater-brown hair. So he said, "And I did, I went up there, and I looked at them. And right in front stood an older man, with a white beard. He was maybe a rabbi or something; he had a big cape." And he was telling this to all these officers. He was very emotional about it.

And he said, "I stood there. I was supposed to shoot them all. And the old man, with the white beard, he looked at me with eyes that said, 'You, young man, what did I ever do to you?'" He says, "I just couldn't do it. And I hesitated, and the commanding officer, he said, 'If you think you're going to save them, you're not, because if you don't do it, the others here will. They're instructed there waiting. So, you're supposed to do that. That is your test. And if you don't do it, they will do it and shoot you, too.'"

He was telling the story; I was all ears. And then everybody was silent.

And then the one man that's in the meeting, he said, "Did you shoot them?"

He said, "Yes."

"Ah," he said, "Good." He did, so he's in.

And I heard that and I understood. I pictured the old man with the gray hair. And to this day, still the way I saw it in my mind.

So my mother wants to raise the atmosphere, and she says, "Now, my little daughter is here and she wants to say a little poem for you. And she's under the table here."

My father almost died.

So, when she gives me the word, and say, "Lieber Doktor Pillermann, see der mal mein Püppchen an. Doll needs you." And I take a curtsy. We always had to take curtsies.

So I went out, but not all the way out. While I was still walking over, I heard the one man say,

"Did she understood all that?"

My father says, "No, she's too young. She's too dumb. She don't understand." That hurt my feelings so that's why I remember.

The young man started crying. He started to sob. And then I left the room. And so, that was the end of that story.

Days later, my mother asked my father, "What happened to the young man that was crying here?"

He says, "Oh, short process," which means they shot him, right after that, somewhere.

It's a short process.

So, that's a bad story, I'm sorry, but it is a true story. I think it's important that children know these stories.

2- Dr. Pillerman

CHAPTER 3

CHILDREN LOVE A PARADE

We lived upstairs in this apartment and a parade was coming down the street. The parade was all Hitler Youth and other uniformed young people. To me, they were pretty big like teenagers, also adults.

And the parade with the flags, with the drums, singing, marching, singing military songs. You couldn't avoid it because they were on the radio; they were everywhere. And so you see them coming along and in their uniforms with the flags.

So the big parade is right in front of my house going by in the street. And, as I learned later, you had to go. If you worked somewhere in some office they come and say, "There's a parade coming by the street and, what's-your-name, I want you down there at that time."

And one person in your office is assigned to go and check. You check in with that person on that corner. And if you're on the list and you didn't come, it's not good. So that's how it worked all throughout and the Communists did that too, later.

And I'm a kid, we know the songs already, because we hear them on the radio, seen other parades or heard them.

"Da-dam-da-bum-bum-ba-da-drum-da-drum-da-dum." The drums, they're stimulating for children, "Ta Dah!"

We skip along and we go, "Yay!"

And adult people who were standing there, they were made to dress up with their nice coats on and their little foxes over it. And they're standing and they didn't show emotion, which, thinking about it, they hated that. But they had to go or you lose a job; supervisor's there.

And I'm with at least four or five other kids my age. We skip along with the parade. We know some of the songs. We're singing along, and we're laughing, and we're just having a good time because it's music and it's rhythm and that's all we know.

My mother, looking out the window, yells, "Ingrid, get up here!"

And some people, "Yes," mad at me, "why are these kids making a racket?"

We were happy because we hear the music, that's all. But I don't know what they were thinking. To this day, I think why did they look so angry at us for having a good time? The parade is there for the public to see.

Well, anyway, my mother finally made it down the stairs, and then she came and she grabbed me by the hair and she pulled me and she spanked my butt, "And every time you see a parade coming, you go home!"

And other adult people who were watching said, "Yeah, that's right." They agreed that I needed a spanking because we enjoyed the parade.

We didn't think about the politics, but you see what I mean to say is all parades, big music, big drums, I never understood.

"Deutschland, Deutschland über Alles in Erde. Schwarzbraun muss mein Mädel sein." which means, "Black and brown my girl must be." I don't know why it is. That was the words of this one song. Uh, it makes no sense to me. At the time, I wouldn't know. It was a song and it has rhythm, and I know the words and we could sing along.

All the adults that were watching the parade, which obviously now I understand were made to go and watch the parade, why did they agree that we had the spanking coming and we should not skip along, and sing along?

Question, I still have that question.

CHAPTER 4

MURDER AT THE STREETCAR STOP

This incident, in Berlin, it had to be before 1942. It probably was '41. I was going somewhere with my mother. We wanted to ride the streetcar. We stood on the stop. And we were still waiting for it. It was fall, and it was cool; people were wearing coats. The men choose nice coats—you know, people dress very well in the big cities. There was a bunch of people and it was the hour when people get out of the office, like six. And we're standing there, waiting for the streetcar.

Suddenly, a car comes driving up, a truck-type car and a bunch of armed soldiers come out with big coats with fur collars and they had rifles.

And they say, "Passport! Passport!"

You couldn't go anywhere without your ID, your passport, which everybody knows, so everybody has it. And they show their passports, and if they were Jewish, there was a Jewish star in a kind of paler print over the whole page, to show this is a Jewish person.

So, anybody who had the star had to go step over further into the stop. The stop had a roof for the rain. And My mother suddenly realized, *danger*. I didn't understand that; I was just looking.

She grabbed me and she says, "Let's go!"

And we go around the corner right behind us to go into another street, and she ran with me into the street and we hear shooting starting, "Po, po, po, po, po, pop." We hear screaming of at least one or two women voices.

My mother stops and says, "Oh my God! They're killing all those poor souls!"

And then she starts crying and we run, run, run, run, to the next corner so we get around the corner away from their view. So we go around and an old man come walking up.

My mother said, "They're shooting all those poor people," then she was crying.

And the man says, "Don't let them see you cry."

And she said, "Oh my God, we are not going to go back." So, we walked across the street for several stops, and I kept thinking, "Wow? How far are we going to walk?" That's what I'm thinking because

I know the streetcar comes all the time. She didn't want to go back to that street. We walked for a long time, and I was so tired.

And then she said, "Well, I guess it's ok now."

So we went back to that street and wait for next streetcar. She had cried, and then we went home.

Days later, my father came home and my mother was telling the story.

And he says, "Well you don't have to get hysteric and cry because you're getting yourself in danger. They were just Jewish people! It's the Jewish problem." And I remember that exact words. He said, in German, the "Jüdischesproblem".

And then he says, "That is now the final days to solve the Jewish problem."

I was told to get out of the room. My mother was talking to my father.

He said, "You can't let them see you cry. You can't say anything about it. Just don't get everybody in trouble! You've got to control yourself."

That sort of thing I still heard him say.

4- Murder at the Streetcar Stop

CHAPTER 5

FAMILY ABDUCTED

It was already cold. It was not snow, but people wore fur coats already. I was walking along the first block. There was some Jewish people living in a townhouse that has little grass in the front, very nicely kept. They owned the shipping company, and they had a big backyard behind, with big barns where all the big trucks were. So they were making good money; they were well-to-do and working very hard. They were busy people. You always heard them yell when the big trucks leave. There were husbands and wives and there were children, too.

I'm walking by, and there's other people accumulated already at their main gate, where the trucks come out. I walked by, and I saw people standing there and staring at that house, and the windows, and the people walking in and out.

5- Family Abducted

And the SS has some cars parked on the side, on a curb, and they are hurrying the family up, and they're loading stuff in their cars like if you go on a big trip. They're taking their bedding.

In Germany, people use featherbeds, big sacks loaded with feathers, and they are very soft, and they're very warm. So, it's common; everybody has them. These people had brand new ones, and nice, and big, and fluffy. And I could see that, and they had wrapped them together with the clothesline and made 'em smaller. And they brought 'em out.

One lady, with the fur coat, she was in charge, obviously. She kept telling the other family members,

"Put it in there! Put it in there! Bring it out here! Bring the other one!"

And then they bring out more big featherbeds. So she made sure they bring it out and don't drop it because it was not snow yet, but the leaves were wet. So she didn't want 'em to fall because they were very spanking clean and nice.

So they put 'em in these cars and the SS get mad and say, "That's too big; you cannot have this stuff. You cannot have it! You don't need it!"

But Mama spoke, Jewish mama, "No! You put it in there!" And so they had words.

So finally an SS officer made them take it all out and he says, "Just throw it in the front yard!"

The front yard used to be grass, and now it was already late fall, and it was kinda wet, and little muddy, but they throw it in the front yard.

The other soldiers put her in the car, and the others, too. That is the moment I came, that they were thrown out and taken away. She had no idea what was happening to her. Poor thing.

And people watched. They say, "Yeah! Take 'em away!" These are yells, out of the crowd, "Get 'em!" Remarks like that. And this is how everyday people are, in order to be "goodie-goodie" with Adolf Hitler, with the Nazis.

And I just stood there, and I did not know about where they are going and all of that. We weren't told, you know. And I felt the unfairness.

One lady pinched me in the side.

She says, "Keep going, child. Keep walking. Where you're gonna go. Just go." So I did. And I did my errand that I had to do.

When I came back, it was all quiet; everybody was gone. The doors were closed, the windows were closed. I was a child, but I know that that was not right. And I go back to my mother and I tell her the story.

She says, "Oh my God. You're so lucky that somebody told you to keep going and not standing there. They would have put you in there too! You don't know what can happen."

And that's how dangerous it was for anything you do. A little errand to go and get something from the bakery or store, something can happen to you on the way.

CHAPTER 6

FIRE IN THE BASEMENT

It was winter, in February '42. It was snow, snow, snow, freezing cold. My mother was in the hospital because she was giving birth to my brother. In Germany then—they don't do it anymore—ten days before she has to be in the hospital. And my father was somewhere Hitler took him. We never really know where he was.

My aunt was performing in Berlin, glamorous. She had to watch me because my mother was in the hospital. And she stayed in a hotel-like apartment. There was a couch and a bed and I sleep on the couch. We went in restaurants and it was just wonderful.

Then we get ready in the afternoon to go to the theater. We had bombings happening; we were used to it. It's like it's going to rain tomorrow, you just didn't pay much attention. As a kid, you're not too much afraid. But, there were a lot of bombings then, going on really bad.

One of the days, that she was performing there, we go down this very busy city street, where the theater is. We're walking fast—she always walks fast—and I hold her hand, almost dragging me. Bombs had hit the night before really hard on that street. All the stores were bombed and were still smoking fire or they were just collapsed, all the stones and the bricks on top of each other.

We walked by a fire going on inside the basement, under the stones. I see fire shining through the stone and I see people from down below it, knocking against the door that is closed.

"Boom, boom, boom."

And I hear that and I see there is fire underneath and the people say, "Open it! Open it for us!"

There were people in there. That was a basement where people from the apartment building had tried to find rescue. But they were in there and it was on fire and they couldn't get out. And they were screaming.

I hear them, women and men voices, and I said, "There are people in there!"

"Let's keep going. Let's keep going!" she said.

And I could not open that heavy wooden doors that people put the coals and the potatoes in, and can't climb up. She with her high heels—I don't think so. I don't know if somebody before had tried to, but everybody rushed and tried to get away. And later we went by; it was quiet.

Then it was in the paper. The bomb had hit, there was a fire inside, and by the time they finally got to it and opened it, all the people were dead.

And I said, "Tante, that's the one we went by and I heard them scream!"

And she says, "Sh, sh, sh, sh. Don't talk. Don't talk." Well her nerves were so shattered, too, and she didn't want to talk about it.

And I keep thinking about that little incident. What could have been done? Could I, five years old, climb up there and open that door? No way! It's heavy wood—planks on top of planks, with big screws through, like barn doors or bigger. But I wanted to. I kept thinking, 'Could I? Could I have done anything?'

And all these people were walking by on the sidewalk and nobody attempted to go up there.

I later realized that everybody was running for their lives themselves.

So that was, um, that was the fire in the basement.

6- Fire in the Basement

CHAPTER 7

DANGEROUS MISTAKEN IDENTITY

My aunt and I go to the theater, and the man in the front always greeted us and he was laughing and he was funny. I remember that, was like coming home. Then I go down with them in the dressing rooms for the ladies. And there was a double-bed-type mattress in the corner and all the ladies put their coats on that because it was snow and ice out there. I sleep on top of that.

"Don't move! That's where you stay." I didn't get to see the show. I wanted to, though.

But there was a special big day—special invitational audience. And I don't know nothing about it. And so I dressed up my nice white blouse, red checkered skirt, and a little red bow tie. And she said I can watch the show. She's going to bring me in before the audience comes in. But I have to sit

7- Dangerous Mistaken Identity

on that seat all throughout the show, even intermission, and after that, when everybody left the house, she will come out and get me.

So I was sitting there, and we don't know when the bombs are going to hit. But I sat through many shows where it went "brrrrrrrrrrrr" and the lights blink—they just say, "Stay here."

I remember people looking very worried, but it didn't matter where you go—the worry was the same, you know—might as well stay there. Anyway, it never did hit the theater.

It turned out that the special audience was all big Nazi pigs. The whole house was all SS, Gestapo people, and their lovers, wives, whatever. The women wear a silver fox and nice clothes for the show. The women used to braid their hair; this shows they're German from the olden days.

And so I sit on my seat that I was assigned to, was only three or four rows from center stage—good ticket. I sit there and I look forward. I always loved the time when the orchestra is tuning the instruments.

Anyway, the seats go up in the theater, and I'm not heavy enough to hold it down with my legs, so my legs go up, too. Next to me, the people all coming in, in their uniforms, their medals, and they all want to be so special. I was not impressed because I was used to that: my father and all his "colleagues," so to speak.

Anyway, I'm sitting there and then next to me sits a lady. She is a very pretty young lady. And she has a nice silver fox over her. She has a little crocheted cap that they used to wear in those days. In front of me is a lady has lots of little pigtails, elegantly entwined in her hair. So I'm watching this while I'm sitting there.

And the lady looks back to me, "Ah, hello! You don't have anybody?" But I didn't tell 'em that somebody I know is in the show.

So the woman on the side, she has the silver fox around—they're black and then silver-white tips, which was then used by people who can afford it. So she was sitting there and the hair from the fox tickles my arm, but I don't mind. I keep petting it because it's like an animal. And then I smile at her and she smiles at me.

Then she says, "Look at me again." I look at her.

Then she turns and she talks to her drunk boyfriend. He had the brown shirt with the leather cross; he had the little hat pushed back. He was from the Gestapo, like a beginners Gestapo guy. He was not a big officer, he was just a Gestapo. Anyway, she talks to him,

'whisper, whisper, whisper.'

Then he says, "Look at me," and I looked at him.

Then he gets his henchmen, the SS in the black uniforms with silver, and they point to me. And the whisper goes around, and they want to get me out of there. And I don't know what's going on; you know, I'm barely five years old. I looked back, 'What's going on back here, all the people are talking?'

One man, also in one of those pillbox hats with some medal on—he feels very important. I'll never forget. He had wire glasses, and he was not big of stature. He stood up, really loud,

"That is too much expected of us—to sit here in this theater with a Jewish child!" I had no idea what it meant.

They all whisper-whispered. And that little lady with the grey hair she looked at me and she says, "Don't look back there. Look forward!"

And her husband give her an elbow and told her to stop looking back at me; he was also in some uniform like Hitler.

I don't know what's going on, but I knew it wasn't good. And now everybody was staring.

So, two men in civilian clothes—they were from the theater—they say, "Are you with one of the entertainers?"

And I said, "Yeah!"

The one man run back.

So here comes my aunt. They got her out of the dressing room. She's wearing full stage makeup, full costume, but she put her coat over. Underneath the coat, all the fluff was peeking out. She goes through, people stand up so she can walk in, and then suddenly she stood next to me.

She says, "Mützieschin," that was my nickname. And she says, "Mützieschin, come with me," and I stand up.

I say, "But the show hasn't started yet! I want to see the show!"

"Another time," she said, "Let's go."

So we went out to the main walk on the side, and she walked with me, and another SS officer came who was friendly to her. She was beautiful, and she had a lot of admirers. So he guided us to backstage.

And I keep saying, "But the show!"

He said, "Never mind. Another time." And he didn't talk to me; he didn't tell me nothing going on.

The following day, my mother had already given birth, and she brought me home. My father was there, my mother was there, and all of them were very mad.

7- Dangerous Mistaken Identity

I remember my father yelling. He says, "How can you take this child among all these Nazi pigs?"

She said, "I didn't know they would look at her as a Jewish child!"—just because I had dark brown eyes.

Well, that is true; nobody thought that either.

But he says, "They are unpredictable and you have no idea what they're capable of!" He said, "It could have been minutes after that! If the Gestapo would have taken her out, she would be in that car, she'd be on the train, she'd be at the concentration camp"

Well, she didn't know, she didn't mean harm.

My mother was crying and they all yelled,

"You'll never see her again! She's not allowed to come back here!"

Terrible. She just dashed out of there.

I was so devastated, "When can I see Tante?"

"Oh! Don't even talk about it!"

So, from there on, the war continued.

CHAPTER 8

WAITING IN LINE FOR BREAD

I was first grader. I had to start school, and so I'm staying with my grandmother in Biesenthal—because the school was less attacked than a school building in Berlin.

My mother was in Berlin, at the apartment, with my baby brother, and she was trying to see if we can make it. My father is somewhere, wherever Adolf takes him. Well that didn't last very long because the war was getting hard, and the bombing was every night, and it was dangerous.

So I went to school. My grandmother picked me up. On the way there were dangers. It could be an alarm could break out, sirens could go off, and where do I go? She would have to be there and be with me, and we can go for the first open shelter—which is basements. If you're in the street you have to go into anything. So you don't go out after dark at all. The slightest light that you might make could get bombs thrown down. So the thing was, keep it dark, no lights. This was this atmosphere.

So in the day, you try to go and do your little shopping if possible, which you don't know. This is small town, suburban, but still, everybody goes to the one baker. The baker bakes in the morning what he can, and when he's out, he's out. And a long line of people will stand outside and make a long snail, we called it, and you better don't cut corners. People punch each other out.

So my grandmother would want to go to the bakery and see what she can get. So I was told when I come out of school, walk over to the line that's outside the bakery and find her, and then stand with her in line. That way she don't have to leave her spot in line, because she definitely wouldn't get it back.

So I come out of school, and I find her in line, and she was not in the front and she was not the way in the back—she was somewhere in the middle. So I stand there with her, in line.

There's a little hunchback Jewish man with the star. He had been there in line since early morning before the bakery opened, so he was maybe the fourth person in line. And then there were some steps to go up into the store.

So, everything went very slow, I suppose, and when he went into the store, suddenly we hear a big tumult, screaming and hollering. People were yelling at each other inside the bakery.

She said, "Stand here." She's going to go and check it out. And she said, "There's this old man, and he says that it's his turn and they tell him to leave, and go to the back of the line," which in the meantime was really long, going around the corner and all.

And he yells and screams, "I've been here since early this morning when everything was still closed, and you're telling me I can't have bread, and I need to leave and go to the back of the line? I'm already handicapped!" And he didn't say it quiet—he screamed it. The whole time he was carrying on.

And then I run over there and see what he's doing. He'd started kicking people. He was so angry at everybody. People don't stand up for him, that's what he meant.

Why don't they speak for him and say, "Yes, he's been here since this morning!"

Nobody said nothing.

Then some, who don't know really—they weren't there in the front—they hear him being pushed further and further back and they go,

"Yes! Go in the back!"

But some of them say to him, "Please, go home. Leave!" He was in grave danger.

My grandmother finally says, "Let's leave. It's becoming too much. Be quiet, don't say anything, and let's go."

We leave. We don't buy bread. We could not take the chance to get in the middle of all that, the SS might be coming. She had me by the hand and dragged me behind and she really hurried.

I keep asking, "Why don't they give him bread?"

She says, "You can't say nothing. You just keep going. Don't look back, just look down, and keep going."

Later, at home, I ask her more, "Tell me why do they that to him? It's not fair. It's not rightful." I remember using that word. He'd been there all the day, and it's fall, it's cold.

She says, "Never mind, just shh."

They always shush me up. They don't explain to me what I want to know. I want to know what's going on, 'Why did everybody be goody-goody with Adolf Hitler, with the Nazis?'

But now I know why: because they would have been put away, too. A lot of the people worried about this old man, because if somebody had already called the SS they would be coming to collect him and maybe more people. That's why my grandmother wanted to leave, even though we didn't had our turn yet.

It was unfair the way he was treated. He did the best he could, being there early in line before the bakery opened. It was not fair and it wasn't right.

8- Waiting n Line for Bread

CHAPTER 9

SCHOOL KIDS ON THE FRONT

My grandmother lived two hours out of Berlin. I got to enroll in their local school, which was a real school building. We weren't bombed, at first. While we were in the school, we had alarms, and we had to go down in the basement, and then they looked how far the bombers were passing. Berlin is not far, and when the bombers went over to Berlin to bomb, and something happened that they couldn't drop all their bombs, they gave them command to come back and, "Just drop the bombs out of the way."

In the morning, when we get to school, all the grades come together in this courtyard. We have to all assemble, and we all have to stand up and look at this flagpole in the middle. Hitler Youth, boys that are a little older, pull the rope and get the flag up which was, of course, the swastika Hitler flag.

And then we had to do this thing, just like they do in America, and you sing a song or you say something, "I pledge allegiance to the flag…" Well, over there it's a different saying, of course, but it is the same thing; you pledge allegiance to this flag, and to that regime, and you had learned the first verse of the national hymn, which was played. We have to sing it. I hated that. I hated the idea of putting the flag over everybody. And I was a very shy child; I would never say anything, just scared.

So that's how my first grade went until the school collapsed because of a bomb. Then I had no more school, and forget that flagpole in the middle. I hate, to this day, flag-waving, because I think it's totally unnecessary.

Hitler youth: 10-year-olds. They were told this was good for the boys. And they learned the songs, and they go to camp and all stuff that Boy Scouts do. Pretty soon they were walking in parades, they were holding flags, and then, another bit down the road, they were actually sent out to the war, and many were killed.

And I knew one, that I met later. He was already, by that time, a young teenage boy. He had medium blond hair, but he had a white-blond stripe of hair right through the middle, very obvious.

So naturally you say, "How come you have the white hair like that?"

And the boy explained: He was 10 or 11. He was sent to the war, his best friend standing next to him, and they wearing the Hitler youth uniform. They were sent somewhere; he didn't know where it was, somewhere in the country.

And he said, "We stood there. We were shaking; we were afraid; we were crying, and we did not know where to go and what to do."

They were on a wagon, and they're supposed to shoot. He says all he knows is they were caught by the Russians. And they made them all get off the wagon and stand in the field, and then they shot them. And his best friend was shot and killed, right next to him—that second his hair turned white.

And I later saw other people having that. Then I learned that when you have a real shock like that happen, that your hair turned white. And I don't know how he got away later. And he actually came back to Berlin, where he was from, originally.

9- School Kids on the Front

CHAPTER 10

GRANDMOTHER'S NEIGHBORHOOD

On the way home from the bakery and shops, and from the school, we had to walk a main street. It has big trees on both sides, and there's traffic in the street.

My grandmother had me; I was holding her hand as we were walking along that street. There were a bunch of people walking on the sidewalks. There was a light, so you had to wait on a red light. All the people stood there and waited for the light to change, like anywhere else.

Next to us, on my left side, a car stopped also. Grandmother was on my right and next to her was a lady. She had her daughter with her; she was a bigger child than me, probably ten, twelve. She was very quiet type of girl. They all were quiet, waiting for the light to change.

And the car next to us on the left-hand side stopped because of the red light. There were four young men in there, in the Nazi uniform: the yellow-brownish shirt had a little hat of some sort, and uniform-like. They all were sitting in there, and they were doing whatever they were told to do.

Next to me, on my right side, was this lady with this girl and they had the yellow star on their sleeve.

Everybody was silent, and suddenly they opened two doors and out came two young men—one from the back seat, one from the front seat. And they run over and they grabbed the mother and pushed her into the car. She screamed; the girl screamed too, which was very bad for her. Then they punched the lady, blood spraying all over the glass.

I was just staring at it, afraid, and the light changed. And everybody tried to run—not run, but walk fast. Pretend you're not scared of them.

And the girl was making motions to go toward the car and screamed, "Mama!" real loud. And I never forgot it; it just went through me like electricity.

The other people that were on the sidewalk, they say, "Child, be quiet. Child, keep looking forward. Keep going."

Two men opened the car door again and came out again, and the mother screamed, "Keep going! Keep going!" from inside the car.

But they came out, the two of them, and they grabbed her daughter. The light changed and they speeded off. Just "choo" disappeared.

My grandma holds my hand, tighter, saying, "Keep walking. Keep walking. Keep looking down. Don't talk. Just keep going."

I felt the danger because everybody was very tense. I understood it was not the right time to ask, but I was full of questions. We all just kept walking fast to get away from there. We had to walk another two blocks or so to the house.

When we got in the house I asked, "What were they doing? Why did they take them in the car? Why did blood go all over this window?"

I was told to hush up, don't talk, don't ask questions. And I kept wondering more. Every time something happened like that I wondered more.

Shortly thereafter, in this time, the planes had come into Berlin and they want to drop the bombs and so they just drop them in the country out there. The sirens go off and you hear, "Boom, broom." The ground shakes. If it would've hit, you had it. And we sit in the basement until it stops.

All the other houses—across the street, and on our side and down the other way—were bombed. Everything was on fire. All of them. Only my grandmother's house was not. We had a little forest right next to us, and maybe that's what kind of made them not really see the house well.

But there were fires all down the street. And across the street, a lady had put her laundry out and it was still hanging on the line. And now she was grabbing it and her house was on fire and she screamed, screamed like she is on fire.

And my grandmother, and later my father said, "This is stupid woman, to hang white clothes on a clothesline when planes come because they see that." And so that's why the neighborhood got bombed.

It really scared me. And my mother heard about it and the following day she showed up very nervous. She grabbed me and everything that belonged to me and we were gone.

CHAPTER 11

THE BUNKER

My brother was about two or three and we were in Berlin. We lived in the second floor, up in an apartment building in Tempelhof. All our windows hung with black paper so not even a needlepoint of light coming out.

Every night, my mother insisted go to sleep like normal: put on pajamas and go in your bed. But when we are having an alarm, that is very, very loud—everybody will hear it—we're going directly putting on our clothes, including a winter coat, and hats, and gloves, and everything. And we have a little suitcase standing by the front door that she will grab, plus my brother and a blanket. Then we go on a corridor and we go down the stairs, and then from there, we will go to the bunker. Normally, all the other people have short-cut that—the kids are fully dressed. They all come down the stairs, and they all rush over to the bunker.

11- The Bunker

By now the sirens had doubled the sound, it just don't go just 'ju, ju, ju', goes loud and frequent, goes 'je-ju, je-ju'.

We were never done because, by the time that they had to close the bunker doors, they give this extra-loud sound and you can't get in anymore. And now you are exposed to the bombs. My mother exposed us to that every night because she would not accept,

"Not my kids! They're not going to go to sleep with their boots on and everything! They are going to sleep in their pajamas!" So that was deadly, really.

My mother was, of course, nowhere near ready with us. She would dress the little toddler brother. It was cold usually; our heaters cooled down by that time at night. It is freezing cold—you see your own breath inside the house.

And I would, "Br, br, br, br, br, br, br, br, br, br," shake. I was so nervous. I was incapable of even thinking, 'I have to put the coat on. I have to close the button.' I was just so nervous, so scared.

And she would yell at me, "Put on coat! Get it on!"

And then she would have to come over and help me because I was incapable—I was just standing there shaking.

By the time she gets us all around, we go downstairs—thank God the bomb had not hit yet. We're going across the street. She has a *Fieze*. That's a little flashlight, not with a battery. You press a button and it goes, 'pree, pree, pree, pree, pree,' and it makes light, badly, but it does make some light. We have to put our hands across it so you just see a little red light coming through your fingers. You no longer can have a light because they would shoot at you.

We get there; we go down the stairs for the bunker, and it's all barricaded. And we're out there and trying to ring the bell and the men that are watching the door inside, they yell at my mother. They let us in and they close the bunker. All the people have been in the dark until they get us through the door in and close it again and then they all yell at my mother. And of course, I feel I'm being yelled at, too. You go in this room. All the way along the wall there is wooden benches. People make a little room and we sit down.

Other kids were in bunk beds in some other rooms inside the bunker. If the parents pay a certain amount of money a month, then you get these bunk beds for your children. And you bring 'em every night and they sleep right away, alarm or no alarm. It's very hard to get a sleepy child to stand up and do something.

All these mothers bring little toys and little things for the little ones, and they throw them all in the

11- The Bunker

middle of this big room. There is a bathroom; you can go to toilet.

The alarm is out there, raging. And I'm just sitting, dizzy. So dizzy, so, so tired. Sometimes we feel hardly anything, but mostly it was quite a lot and sometimes it was really scary. Adults start crying and whimpering.

This bunker was built very scientifically, very deep in concrete box. And it has steel chains and hooks tied onto the walls, called a hanging bunker. Shakes like a ship, but it doesn't break, and so it's a very safe bunker.

Some of the bombs you hear, they go, 'eeeeeeeeeee,' until you count five, 'boom!' So it comes down with that whistle sound, then it's silent, and then it explodes.

When we come out of the bunker, the sirens make a different sound, 'weebum, weebum, weebum.' That means the alarm is over; you can go home. So then they come out and they go to the house. If they have a house, still—that's a big "if."

And my mother would say, "Don't whine around before it's necessary. Maybe they never did bother your house."

My mother would run the show. She would say, "Let the children go first! Let the children run! And when they get to the corner and they stop, then you know your house is not there."

And so we run, and we skip. When we get to the corner, I would see my street. Our building is there and we keep skipping.

She says, "Alright, everything is fine."

We'd do that routinely. My mother will make good humor and try to keep the people happy, but this is a very, very tense time.

11- The Bunker

CHAPTER 12

RED SKY NIGHTS

One time, we run to the corner and all the children were quiet, just stood there. Instantly all the women start whining and wailing behind us.

And I just look around, "Oh my God, what..."

Mother just grabbed me and says, "Let's go back to our house."

So we go right to our apartment. On the corner, the whole building down—and there's three stories—all of those apartments were open like a dollhouse; it's open for you to put your hands in and play. I see the furniture and the beds with the bedspreads and all, hanging out. It just collapsed. They had some bombs that do that, they just collapse the building without fire. Whole blocks—all of it—down. No humans were hurt because they were all in the bunker.

But we look out, it's still night sky, we see the sky all lit up from fire from the next town or next part of town and Berlin is a huge city. And you just stand there with your mouth hang open. I didn't get to look too long because I was ushered away, "Quick, quick, quick, quick!"

Our front door was gone! Our apartment, inside, my mother's door to the bedroom was standing on the bed. It flew across the whole room and put itself standing up!

We said, "Oh! There's the door! Wow!"

My mother was showing everybody, "Look at that! How did it do that?"

And my father later explained and said it was the air pressure 'chooo!' took it out of the hinges and put it on the bed, leaning against the wall. If you would have been in there: that would have killed you, right there, flying out through.

All the windows were gone in our entire place—not just ours, everybody's. There was no such thing as glass anymore. Winter gets really cold there, so everybody's thought is, 'How am I going to close the windows, somehow?' Which was the thing to do and it was very difficult. You climb around in all the other bombed-out houses and you hope to find something you can use to keep the cold out. Find some wooden planks or cardboard. Forget everything else.

Water just comes out the wall, 'ssssssss,' from pipes that were exposed. Which we thought was funny. But the gas would burn. The fire department, which was too busy to really function, they would plug pipes.

Then there was no water. Our street still had some old-fashioned pumps that have been built in 1800's. Good thing they did because that is for emergencies. You can go up there with a bucket and get some water, for drinking, for anything. It's city-water-type-thing.

I had to stand in the line. You stay all day, so family members take turns. I hated that. I mean, what kid likes to stand in one spot for hours? Gee whiz. Just stand there two, three hours, then a brother or a mother or somebody comes and takes your turn. And then, after so and so many hours, you have another turn, and that goes on and on and on. So we would have to go through that for five years. And that was for the lucky ones with a water line was not interrupted by bombs.

Some of these bombs, they were acid bombs. So, there comes a man with a woman: she has a coat on; she has a shawl around her, and a man walking her has a hat and he holds it in her face.

I'd been told, "Don't look! Don't look!"

But, I have a look. The woman, her whole face was eaten away by acid. And you could see all her teeth and eye sockets only, like a skull. It was gray, burned-blistery all over. They rushed by us.

It got so bad that, shortly after that incident, all the garden summer houses across the street were all bombed, were all burnt down because they were from wood.

I felt I got education—not by word—but I learned something that's happening. And I want to know what in the world is happening? Of course, I didn't understand the politics, but I understood, there is danger: you can get hurt; you can get killed. People do get hurt and killed and houses destroyed.

CHAPTER 13

HERR TÜCHLER'S QUIET ESCAPE

I really loved Herr Tüchler. Good friends, you know, neighbors. He particularly was such nice Jewish man, older already, retirement age, and his sister even older—an old lady, like me, I guess, now.

They were very neat people, very neat, and had good taste. Beautiful furniture, valuable items in their apartment; no junk. This is not the Woolworth's generation. Ha,ha,ha! That came later!

He was very quiet, nothing to say except, "Hello. Nice day. Goodbye."

So the Jewish thing was on. They were picking people up from their apartments and shipping them out on the trains. In the middle of the night, you hear the big boots. They come up the stairs, and they put their foot against somebody's front door 'boom!' and they rip the door out of its hinges and go down. And then they go in and get the people and leave with them, the way they are. And this was known.

So my mother was thinking. My mother worried about the Tüchlers. So, one time when my father came back, my mother asked my father, trying to be nice because she knows he might get really mad at her.

She says, "Please find out if the Tüchlers are on the list. I want to warn them. When will they come and get them?"

And he had access to those lists. I mean, this is before computers, they were pretty organized. And I remember him telling, "It's very soon." But more than one day; it was maybe a week or two.

So, my father, he says he wants to be gone, he don't want to be here, and, "If you help the Tüchlers escape, you make sure that not one item from his apartment is going into ours. Nothing, and you know nothing, nothing, nothing!"

So, I remember the day when she went over to tell him. She told me not to follow her but I was watching. So she went and, 'knock, knock, knock,' Herr Tüchler let her in. They closed the door; she was in there for a while. And then they come out, and she would not tell me, of course. No, I was just a stupid kid; that would be the worst thing: to tell your kid. But I want to know what's happening, always curious.

They did it very clever. He and his sister had a little suitcase each—maybe it's like a briefcase, almost, but a little fatter—and that was all they were allowed to bring. And I don't know the underground, how it worked. The underground was a big secret. I didn't even know it was called that; I learned that afterward.

Anyway, so, they left with that, and they had their fall clothes on: coat and hat and shoes and nice—they were always nicely dressed. And they left. And you would never suspect that they are running away because they had nothing with them except a little briefcase—you could be going to work somewhere.

In the night, I woke up because you hear people start walking a little bit. They try to be on their socks and really quiet, but the wooden floors underneath, "cr, crack" you hear little scrunchies noises. Me, you know being all aware and listening, I open my door and I went and I saw.

Herr Tüchler had a beautiful, very, very delicately-made pirate ship—a Kogen we call it—those big ships the pirates used to have, with the jolly roger on top. All the lines, and sails, built by somebody. He wanted us to save that. That's going to get us all in trouble, so we can't. Everything has to stay at his apartment.

13- Herr Tüchler's Quiet Escape

So, anyway, he disappeared, nobody knew,

"Oh, I haven't heard?

"Herr Tüchler, is he there?"

My mother says, "He's there, he just keeps it quiet."

So that took a little while.

And then one night, I was told to stay in my room. She says, "Now, don't come out your room! If you hear noise tonight, don't come out."

"Blah, blah, blah," strict advice.

My father was there. He knows what day that was, and they knew before they will be there 2:30 in the morning—and definitely they were.

And my mother already in the corridor, "Here they come with German punctuality!"

And exactly on the right day and time they came. One officer and two other soldiers, and they came up, they rung the Tüchlers' bell, nobody answers. He rung again, nobody answers. And the guy who's trained with his boot, to 'choo!' bang in the door and that's when everybody heard it. The door lands face down on the floor, and they march in there. And they walk around in there. And the officer steps outside and my mother opens our door and she says,

"Look at that!" She points at the sign. We have the brass sign—that was our protection—that says this is an SS apartment: don't bother the people—do not knock here. For other SS to know not to bother this man in here: he is an officer.

She says, "Do not touch this apartment!"

"Well, where is your husband?"

"He's here." He was in the bedroom in the bed and they wear their nightclothes. And they have robes. It's always cold there.

I came out of my room. I saw my father come out in his full SS uniform.

My mother says, "You're crazy! Take it off; you were sleeping in bed! Take it off! Put your robe on!" He had his hair all nicely combed; she took her hands in his hair. She said, "You're coming out of bed! What're you doing with this?"

And he did it: he went back and he real quick, you know, put the robe over. They're so scared. Stupid, but that would be a giveaway.

So, "We don't know about the Tüchlers. They're gone for long time."

My mother even said, "You want to come and look? We don't have fine stuff like that."

And they looked at everything and they didn't take nothing. And we didn't had anything of theirs and that was very important. That was it.

Then the landlord came and put a big board across their broken door, leaned it on there and nailed it. It was like that, the whole war and after the war. Nobody ever went inside and nobody ever stole Herr Tüchler's stuff. It was untouched.

We stuck out just little further before we run away ourselves because it was too dangerous—you know, too much bombing.

CHAPTER 14

RUNAWAYS

My mother finally had it and we left Berlin. Not just her—a lot of people already had packed up and went to the countryside with their little wagons. We load anything in very necessary and then go. You don't know where you're going; you just go.

So then we went on a train and that's when I saw the gate, 'Arbeit Macht Frei.' My mother stood up in the train, looking by the window, and she said to the other people on the train, "I hope they're going away from that."

I don't know what's the matter with that place. I never understood until later. Then we heard a "vroom, vroom vroom vroom," the train changed the other way. It was supposed to be, but at this time you don't trust nothing.

14- Runaways

I remember my mother, standing up, saying, "Oh! Thank God!" I remember the moment because it was so intense.

We visited a lady that had two children and they were older than me. She had taken them right across alongside of the concentration camp. When we visited, they sit outside the little house talking. And she has coffee and cake. It was very close to the concentration camp; I saw the big chimneys with black smoke coming out. It stunk.

The other lady said, "The smell sometimes gets unbearable so I'm going to leave here. I'm not going to stay here any longer. I'm already making arrangements."

And I heard that, and then they looked at me and they said, "You sit over there with your toys and your stuff."

So I had to go to another spot and play with this other kid in the sand. I didn't understand what was going on and I always want to hear.

So we had afternoon there with the coffee cake and then we left. We didn't stay there at all. But my mother was searching for a place and the lady had given her some advice of some other places.

Then we went to the countryside—which everybody did. We went to every little village we heard of, trying to find a place. You go into the farms and you see already the wagons outside, baby carriages and all.

And you ask, "You have a room?"

"No. We have the whole Berlin in here!"

Ha ha ha!

So that was usually the answer. It was very difficult, very difficult.

So, we had tried some people by the seaside. We went to the East Sea in a little hotel. The man was very mean; he would not allow anybody to even make a cup of coffee.

My brother was a baby, and my mother said, "I just want to warm up a bottle for the baby. He would not allow it and evicted us from there because she made the baby bottle. I was there listening to that screaming match.

Then we tried some more places. We wound up in Flötz, and we start walking around farms and just knocking on the doors. So we wandered around, and we wound up in this one farm.

A big, fat farm woman said, "Okay." She had a room in the attic and that's where we stayed.

14- Runaways

CHAPTER 15

THROWING BREAD AT TRAINS

I was seven, maybe going eight. In the law at the time, you had to be seven to go to first grade. Dieter was the same age. Blond, very blond, little, very German-looking country kid. And we went to the same school.

When school was over, we walked together back the same direction. When we walked back, we walked by first where Dieter lives. And the house was a normal little house, by the railroad track. It had a little yard around and little country setting, so they had small animals and garden. Lots of chickens running around and rabbits. I liked to touch the new little chicky-babies when they come out, and the cats. No big animals.

Our farm had big animals. We had cows, and oxen—you know, male cows had to pull the plow, and some hay wagons when they come in with all the hay in the fall. They were real working farm; it was not a ranch, like American-style ranch with acres and acres. But it had acreage and it was growing wheat and oats. And they also had cabbages, lettuce, and potatoes—a lot of potato fields.

So kids, they always create something to play; we would have a good time there. The outdoors and animals and all—it was wonderful, really. We, as kids, play in the wheat fields. To us, we're children, you know the size of seven-year-old, but the wheats are growing really big. They're yellow and they're really like in a jungle. So we run around in there, play catch, hide and seek, and you can't see nobody so you have to listen to the noise of the steps, of the "whoo, hoo," and you go there and there's nobody there.

When we did that, we walked through and we often step a lot of wheat down. The farmer finds out and gets furious. We got scolded a lot because we stomp 'em flat. We get all kind of punishments: and one of them is go and straighten it out if you can; one is get a spanking from your parents, which I got plenty. Dieter was not allowed to come around for a while.

Well, because of that, was one of the reasons why I go over to their farm, which was just a garden and by the railroad track. The husband was employed by the train company. He had to manually put the levers in to change the tracks from straight to going around and back from around to go straight. And he was supplied with this house by the train company.

And when the trains come by we don't hardly look at them. There were güterwagen—that means freight wagons, where the big two doors meet in the middle. And then sometimes the wagons come by with people sitting inside who have a ticket says third class, second class, first class. If there was another train just before, the wagons sometimes slow down to rearrange the tracks in a different direction. He didn't let us come up there where that happened.

But then the Jewish transport trains came. I didn't know at all what's in these wagons. They were freight wagons. They had no windows. They had the big two sliding doors. On the top, underneath the roof, was a board missing on each corner. That missing board was not a window—it could not open or close—it was just gone, on purpose. The big transport trains stopped for a few minutes, maybe five minutes and in that time he was setting the tracks.

Dieter's mother knows the train comes at a certain time. She would tell me, "Come after school. Just drop off your satchel, and then come right over—we're gonna play here."

15- Throwing Bread at Trains

So, I run over—I had to hurry. I tell my mother, "I have to go there. I promised I'd be there."

So, I run over and I remember her standing there already and saying, "There you are! Come on! Hurry! Get in here, get inside the house!"

She had Dieter in there, and she had the basket of heels of bread. She cut off all the heels and then she put them in the basket. She says, "I like for them to be a day old, so they have weight to it."

She says, "Now, there gonna be a freight train coming in, and he's gonna stop right here in front of our house." Up a little bit is her husband setting the track to go toward the concentration camp. "And so when they come and the train has stopped, and you hear 'eeeeeeee'—the metal on the metal— you take a heel of bread and you throw it at the wagon. And the wagon has the big door here closed, but up, right and left, is the board missing and it's open. And there are people in there. And they're hungry. And when you throw a piece and it goes in, and they get that piece of bread, they're happy. So you just throw that."

Dieter was so good; he would have made an all-American baseball player because he'd throw right in. And we'd hear the voices, "Ahhhhh!" and like 'rumble rumble' inside so maybe they all go on top each other trying to pick it up.

But on the front and back of each wagon was a German soldier, in really warm outfits—like a Russian—with a fur hat, long coat, big boots. And they have a machine gun over their shoulder and told to shoot. And their job is to watch that nobody jumps out.

At first, we didn't pay attention to them. We saw them, but we didn't pay attention. We're so used to seeing soldiers and machine guns. That didn't scare you or made you wonder, not when you're seven years old. So, they probably could not believe what they saw.

So then we throw that and then we saw lots of hands coming out—lots of naked, white hands, bony and very white, and they were all trying to get that bread when we threw it. So we'd throw the whole time, as much we could, and Dieter was the one! I'd throw it and it bounces off of the wagon and onto the ground. Dieter was the proud winner.

Then we go, "Yeah! He did it! He did it!"

He was proud that he was so good. He'd keep on doing it really fast and really good. But, we always had a lot left.

So one day, after many days of us doing that every day, a soldier came down, "What are you doing?" And then the other one from the other end came down, too, and he was hitting his machine gun, like 'you get in the house.' Like, 'we'll shoot you if you don't go in the house'—that's what that's supposed to mean. I knew that, but I wasn't afraid of it because I didn't see anybody get shot, at that time.

And so she had us come in, and we hid, and then the train moves on.

Next day, after that, I come running, she's waiting outside—she knows I'm coming running from my farm back to her house—she says, "Shhh, come on in, come inside my house. Quiet."

"Is the train already here?"

Then she told me as we walked into her house, "No, it's gonna be here any minute, so come on in. The soldiers were sent here, and they came in and they were very mad. And they said, 'If we see you again throwing whatever you're throwing, we will come and we get you, and we put you in the train, too.' They told us not to look at them; they're watching."

"Therefore," she says, "when you come here, you gotta come inside the house. We cannot throw bread anymore. We can look at them through the glass windows. However," she says, "you have to stand back at least two feet from the white curtain inside the living room, and then you look and you can see it, but not to be seen." So that's what we did.

And I just thought,

"Wow. That's such a waste of time. I mean, we're supposed to throw bread." Ha, ha, ha. And then later that day, I go home and told my mother.

"You stay home. You cannot go there."

I was deeply hurt. I was really upset that she wanted me to stay home, and not go back there.

She says, "You don't know these soldiers! You don't know how horrible they are! And believe me, you cannot go. It's very dangerous."

I did ask, "Who are these people in the freight wagon? Why they're not sitting in a regular train on your upholstery seat."

"Bad people. Bad people." That's how you talk to kids, 'they're bad people.'

Then, "What? Why? What they do?"

And then I get no answer. And then, when I get no answer, I keep on looking for the answer, and that is why I remember it so well.

So that was the end of our throwing the bread.

15- Throwing Bread at Trains

PHOTOGRAPHS

Baby picture with my Mother

As a toddler before the war

One of my favorite dolls

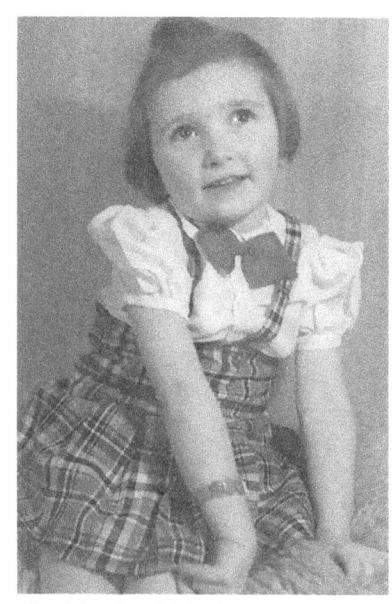

As I looked in chapter seven

Our apartment in Berlin.
Potted plants and broken window glass

Outside our apartment in Berlin.

Sitting on a ruin mound in Berlin

Playing on the top surface of the hanging bunker

Grandmother's house and little forest

"Grandmother"

Brother pulling ladder wagon

Bridge over the river Elbe

Tante Lotte in costume

With Tante Lotte

School photo wearing potato shoes   Foster home clothes

High School   Adult

CHAPTER 16

THE MILK CAN

It must have been 1944 in Flötz, where we were evacuated and living with a farmer. I started school in a very small village, with one room and all the children of different ages together. The older ones, the younger ones were all in rows. I was a first grader.

After a very short time, they said the teacher's gone and got to go to the next village over, which was a three-kilometer walk, and there is another teacher and he will teach you.

"Why is the teacher not there?"

"We don't know; he's gone."

"Okay."

So we went there. The teacher, he was a very nice, skinny man with big, wire glasses, and he had the children from both villages, so he had more children together. He was very mild spoken and we loved him.

And one day, and I don't think it was too long after we just started to learn, write letters, they say, "Well, there's no school today; the teacher is gone."

"Wow, where did he go? Did he get sick?"

"Maybe, we don't know," the adults around there would say, "but he's gone. There is no school. So the next day you got to go to the other village, the other direction," which was five kilometers, "and then there is school, still."

So that's what happened. That walk was five kilometers long on a country road, which is quite a long walk. It was country fields, but it was interrupted by a stretch of maybe two blocks of forest.

We were told, "When you go alongside the forest, go into the forest and walk inside of the protection of the trees until they end, and then go back out on the road and keep going. And if planes come overhead, jump into the ditch where the water runs after rains."

Our farmer had several milk cows, but would not let us have a liter of milk. My mother would argue with him and say, "I have this two-year-old here." She says, "He has to have milk, and you have all these milk cows, so what's the problem?

Just fill the can once a day, a liter. That's all I need for the children!"

They wouldn't do it.

So, my mother gives me little aluminum can, which we used to use in the city to go buy milk, and she says, "When you go to the school, right next to the school is the dairy," where they have cows and they milk 'em and they sell the milk, "and ask them to fill it, and pay them." And she gave me some money.

My mother threatened me at home and she spanked me often and a lot. She said, "Don't you spill any of that milk or you're going to be sorry!"

So every time I have Dieter and some other kid that will walk back with us, and I would ask 'em, "Please, can you wait. Let me go to get milk."

So we all do that and I get the milk. I carry the milk can with my satchel on my back, and we're walking down the road.

Once, there was a bunch of fast-moving Spitfire planes—small planes, come overhead really low-down to us, and shoot at us, "chu, chu, chu, chu, chu, chu, chu." We see them coming and they're going diving toward us and we jump into the ditch alongside the road and it has high grass that has grown wild, and we ditch down and wait for them to pass. They shoot at us.

16- The Milk Can

I have the can of milk. So I only worry about any milk getting spilled. I just worry about that. And I'm down there and I try to cover it and it's just a matter of seconds: we have to jump, we have to ditch down—the plane is already shooting at us. Luckily it never shot us, but it shot my can right in the middle, 'shoo,' through.

Now, the can full of milk was shot through here, and 'juuuu,' two little fountains of milk coming out, and it will go down, down, down to that level and stop.

Oh, I was so scared, 'My mother's gonna beat the heck out of me.' I was so scared. I just prayed, "Please. Dear God, please, please, don't let her spank me." I just prayed and prayed that she won't spank me. No other thoughts of making sense of it. So I was just shaking.

Dieter goes to his house, which is by the railroad track, and I have to walk a little further. I go in and I'm just shaking in my shoes. I bring the can, and I told my mother "It's only half full."

But she sees the hole in and out of the other end, and she goes, "Oh, oh, God! Thank you! You are alright!"

I couldn't believe it, ha! She didn't spank me! Wow! Ha, ha, ha, ha! Only years later understood that she understood what happened. I no longer had to take the can to school.

I don't know, maybe she hold that can under the nose of that farm lady and says, "Look, now. Why don't you give us some milk?" She has all these big, healthy cows in the stable.

Anyway that's just the story of the milk can.

He, he, he, he, he. It's not funny; it's funny now—it's sad-funny, you know.

16- The Milk Can

CHAPTER 17

YOU ARE MY SUNSHINE

On the farm in Flötz, where we stayed, the Germans had built a barricade made of big, huge tree stumps and barbed wires and all of that. This barricade was for tanks not to get through the main street, which was totally ridiculous because there were fields all around, so they could just go around it.

So, now they expected them and here they came. The Americans entered with big tanks, but there was the tank barricade. And so then the Americans took over and with their rifles, they get everybody out, and tell them to take that barricade back down, he he he, which was a huge job.

My mother said, "Don't go outside. Do not be seen there; they will get you to work like that." So we stayed inside.

17- Your are My Sunshine

The Americans came and stayed in different farms. They come and they are fat guys. I never seen fat people. They were nice to us kids. This one of them, very fat guy, and he has all the children go in the barn, sit on the floor and he teaches a song, "You are my sunshine, my only sunshine," he, he, "You make me happy when sky is gray. You never know, dear, how much I love you. Please don't send my sunshine away."

I did not understand one English word, and to this day I remember the song. And he sits there, this fat soldier, with his helmet on, and the tears are running down his face when we were all singing it.

He closed all the barn doors that nobody from the outside could come in, but my mother had, of course, snooped and got them all, "Shhhh, come on, come, come, come, come, come on."

And they open the door and they come and they say, "Sing again!" And so we have to sing this again and they all really loved it. And that was my very first English I learned, ha.

And so while they were on this farm, they saw my mother fighting with the farm woman about giving milk to the children. I mean, we had this little boy, and then there were some other people that were on different farms came because they know they had the cows, and say they want some milk, too. The farm woman, she would not give anybody anything. And this one big soldier would say, "What's the matter?"

And my mother, speaks a little English, explains, "There's all these children. The mothers want milk for the children, but she won't give us any milk."

Whatever he said, that was it. They're milking the cows. My mother says, "These American soldiers are farmer boys; they know how to milk the cows! Let them do it; they will do it right," she says to the farm woman who thinks they don't know.

And so they milk the cows. So, they gave us the milk we needed. The other women and kids who come from other farmhouses where they didn't had big animals like that, bring all kind of containers, and they fill 'em up with milk.

"How many children you have?"

They count them and then they divided it. And they told the farm woman to go in the basement and close the door, ha, ha, ha.

In the stable, there is this Brahman bull because it was sort of winter, not the summer where the animals are out in the field. And he was sort of silver-gray with gigantic hump on the back, and horns, and a blue tongue, I remember the blue tongue. The farmer man was very proud of it. This is not common to have Brahman bulls there.

So these farm guys arranged it, and they butchered the big bull. Ohh! The farmer almost died himself. They did not ask the farmers because they would not give us anything. And so, he told all these families—wives and children and the rest of farmers, too—"Get buckets. Go home, get buckets. Rinse 'em out, bring them."

So they come back with buckets, and they divided this huge animal. My mother was not that good in English, but good enough to get along translating.

When they asked, "How many children you have?" He even wanted to see them.

She said, "Show him how many fingers."

So they gave them enough meat to be able to cook right then and there.

The farm woman screams at the top of her voice all the time, "Ahhh!" insults.

They told my mother to tell her to shut up. So my mother tells the farmers, "Please do not make all that noise; you're endangering us all," because, you know, we're the enemy. "So just don't talk."

The farm woman keeps yelling and screaming so they locked her in the basement underground, where they keep the potatoes over the wintertime. There's steps down; it's all cool; it's dark. The rats run around and some chickens run in there to hide from the winter.

My mother said, "You better be glad you're alive." They make sure they get water they need and other things.

So the Americans thought my mother owns the farm because she was taking this attitude of ownership. They would ask all along while they're there, "Can we have some chicken?"

"Sure!"

And so, after their stay, I don't know how many days—it was maybe a week, or a week and a half—they had consumed all the chickens that they had there. It was a barnyard full.

My mother says, "Americans sure love chicken. So when they want the chickens, they can have the chicken." Every night they were barbecuing with chickens.

So anyway, that was funny, but now there was suddenly a German SS group of soldiers coming.

17- Your are My Sunshine

CHAPTER 18

TEN DAYS IN THE LINE OF FIRE

Now, SS soldiers came in to fight and had a shootout for ten days. The forest was the safest not to get shot. And so, all the farmers and their wives and all run away into that little forest that we used to have to go through to go to school—there was no more school, forget that altogether.

I remember the farmer and his wife had blankets and everything to sleep at night in the forest. And it was late fall or early winter; it was not snow, but it was cold and wet, and moist, and blah.

So my mother says, "Not me, ha, I'm not going in that forest!"

And there was another young woman with small baby. So we're going in the basement of this farmhouse, and so did all of the American soldiers, hiding in there, ready to shoot.

There was a pump in the room and you can drink the water from the pump that's direct from the ground. There was a drain in the middle of the room, so if you have to go to the bathroom, you have to lean over that and pee down in there. We had a smoking chamber in there, where the farmer has been smoking all his sausages and bacon sides and all of that, so there was food. They brought down some hay bales to lie on, and we had our baby mattress from the baby bed. That's all, really. But we didn't sleep because SS soldiers were shooting right at us, at the farmhouse.

My mother, the other Berlin woman with her infant, myself, and my two-year-old brother (who would never stay still) had to lie down along the basement wall—one American soldier, one of us, another soldier. And they had their rifles out of the windows. We were yelled at and punched if we move or talk.

Their commanding officer tells them to go up one by one and then shoot over the garden wall. There was another farm behind us; the SS army occupied that one. The aim was to go and get the SS army to leave the other farm.

As soon as it got dark, they come crawling over and try to shoot at us.

The American commanding officer, he will say, "Try to get over the garden wall."

So we had to be in there real quiet. If we have to go to the bathroom, they announce it to the other soldiers and make it quiet and we have to wait until they say, "Now."

One soldier got shot and he was whimpering and crying, and the other soldiers slapped the heck out of him, 'whack, crack,' "Shut up!" Not supposed to cry, I guess. And they had him on the stairs; I remember watching him all the time, and he was crying and he was sobbing and carrying on. They all get mad at him.

Then a whole group of American Red Cross soldiers came in. I don't know where they came from and how, but there they were. And they are crawling in down the stairs and they get that guy that whimpers, who has been hurt, and they slap him around, too—then they dragged him out of there and disappeared and were gone. I don't know where they came from or where they went.

So the others were still in there; the shooting was going on all night. Their commanding officer will have one or two out there operate machine guns on tripods that move right and left, that go, 'chi, chi, chi, chi, chi, chi, chi, chi, chi, chi, chi.'

They all want not to go there because they shot direct at them. So what they do is they shoot, and then they open the basement door and roll down. They fall down on purpose, quickly, so that the shots following them will not get them and nobody else—we all had to stay down on the floor. And this was every night. Ten days.

While you're lying on the stomach you can't do nothing. And so, my mother and the other woman would pray, pray—and my mother is totally anti-religious, but they were all praying,

"Bu, bu, bu, bluh, please…"

Ha, ha, ha.

Nobody got hurt except the one soldier.

And then suddenly they come back and they say, "Well, there's two of them shot dead, lying right behind our wall."

Then they come back again at another time in this ten days and they say, "There is nobody there anymore and they left their radio behind!" That radio was shot dead and that's why they left it. The Germans know that they'd better get going, so they had quietly run off.

So the Americans say, "That means that Russians are coming!"

As morning came, the farmers that all had hidden in the woods came back.

CHAPTER 19

THE BRIDGE OVER THE RIVER ELBE

In history, this situation is known as the Battle of Barby. Barby is the town closest to the village, Flötz, where we were evacuated. The bridge was built across the river. People could walk across the bridge. On the other side, the bridge had train tracks. Iron boats and freight trains and all used that bridge on a regular basis.

We often did go to the little town of Barby, on the other side, which was more town-like because that had some stores and more. The village of Flötz had none of that. I often walked across that bridge before. But it was dynamited by the Germans to avoid any Russian or American to come in. Totally useless, but they did that, dynamited.

So now the American soldiers, they announce to us that they are gonna be leaving. As they were getting ready to leave and packing up, they told us, "The Russians are gonna come within the day."

The American soldiers had built a whole 'nother bridge, emergency bridge where they could bring their tanks across the river. It's a bridge already kind of made and they just spread it out and put it across, and bring the tanks—you know how heavy tanks are—across the river. All their trucks, jeeps, machine guns and tripods, and soldiers came that way. Now, they have to go back over that emergency bridge with everything and the Russians are waiting on the other side.

And so we say, "Can we come over your bridge with you?" I even personally asked one, "Can we go with you, and then go our way?"

Because we like them—they were nice—and the reputation of the Russians soldiers was horrible. We hear from others who had run away from them and who came through the village; not good.

Well, the Americans, they said, "No. You cannot." They do not allow it because there was some kind of military law. They could not let us go. Not one of us.

They say, "When we go across the bridge, and we have all our equipment across it, then we take it down and take it with us."

So we were stuck.

They said, "You can go up to the bridge, the one that's dynamited, and you can try to see, between the ruins of it all, how you can go across this river." And this was not a creek, it was a river, a fast-moving, deep river, where big ships came through. They said, "So if you hurry, and you go down there, you might make it across and then you run away."

So, everybody that was alive went down to the river, to where the bridge used to start and go over. Well, it wasn't too far for us to walk from our village, but there were others that came from other villages. It was raining hard. It was fall season; I don't know what month but the leaves are wet and mushy. The kind of weather where you don't want to go outside.

So we have to run and we also know that we can only take some blankets and put on all our warmest clothes. All these farmers take ladder-wagon, wooden wagon with metal tires. We call them a ladder, like a ladder where you climb, because on the side is like a ladder. They load everything in there and squish it in. So ladder wagon was very useful for transporting smaller things, too. And everybody had a ladder-wagon, especially on the farms.

But all these farmers came before us and thought they could bring it over the bridge, where people used to be able to walk, which was not possible. Probably what they thought they could do it there because it was just wooden boards, but the other side was railroad tracks—you cannot roll anything on a railroad track.

Well, they had made it up to where the bridge was severed, and the wagons were all standing there, loaded with bedding rolled up tight, and other things that they wanted to bring—personal things, mostly to keep warm.

And the rain comes down. I had lots of clothes on, one on top of the other—so did everybody else. Whatever they had. I remember I had this red, knitted shawl tied around, and it was wet. Everything was wet. And there was really no way to protect yourself and you get colder as you get wet.

The bridge was collapsed into the river, and where it collapsed into the river the water was twirling around in whirlpools. It was scary to look at, and you saw people, "plew, plew, plew," falling into the water. Nobody can save them; they scream one time, it pulls them down, and then they're gone.

Others had run around and looked for any fishing boats or something left, but I remember them—they came back and they said, "There is no fishing boats anymore." Many of them say, "Look, we went up the river, down the river: there is no boats."

And so my mother is up and about, trying to find a way.

CHAPTER 20

CLIMBING LIKE A MONKEY

There was a man, a German man. I don't know where the heck he came from, but he was very agile. He took some children on his back, climbing like a monkey, across all that dynamited bridge. He took little children, and he put them in his backpack with just the head looking out, then he climbed across all of that. He managed like a monkey; he was really agile. And he's made it back, trying to rescue some more.

It is very dangerous because the explosion has taken away the beams that went across the bridge for one meter. The beams were still there except that one place. You have to jump it. And it's raining and slippery, so you're going to be standing there on this beam and you have to jump over to continue.

So he says, "That means I have the rucksack with the baby in it, and I am jumping over, and hope I hit the other side and then quickly try to get my balance, and continue to bring this baby to the other side." And I don't know who picks it up.

When my mother got to him, I was standing next to her. She was trying to give him my little brother.

I heard him, he says, "I can't do any more. I have taken three of 'em and I can't because I'm already too weak now. And when I go there and I jump that one meter with this kid,"—my brother was close to two years old; he was not a very little infant—"I don't think that will be safe. We won't make it." He says, "If we miss it, we go down and we're dead. So now I just have to go and get myself over."

In the meantime, I watch the drama, looking down there, where all the water going, 'shhhh,' people falling, 'chu, chu, chu, chu, chu,' bodies falling all the time, every few seconds.

An example, which made an impression on me, was a young lady. She had an infant, little infant. And the damn thing, she has high-heeled shoes.

So my mother, "Look at that crazy woman! Why did she wear those high-heel shoes?"

And the woman goes up to the bridge with the high heels on and the baby. It was a new baby in her arm, really little baby.

And my mother said, "Look at that crazy woman! Now what in the world is she thinking, going with the high heels?"

And I was just watching, my mouth open, 'My God! She has a baby!' And she had a suitcase—a big suitcase! 'My God! What can she have in there?'

In the one hand, she has the suitcase and then she has the baby the other. And she's trying to hold on the ladder as she goes up. Just before she gets to the top, she was trying to do something about shifting the suitcase or something and the suitcase is heavy, obviously—she has stuff in it—and it kind of pulls her down and so she has to let it go. She let it go and the damn suitcase is falling, good. However, she's very unsure now, she's out of balance, and the baby falls on the other side. She looks at the baby falling and she jumps that way, too—her mother instinct.

And I watched that. I'm just terrified.

And my mother, she says, "Can you climb up that ladder to the top and then walk over and hold your balance, and when you come to this place, jump over the broken part and catch it on the other side, and then continue across the bridge?"

I said, "No. I know I can't do it." And I said to my mother, "I'm not gonna go." A meter is a long thing for a little kid, way up high. I mean—way up high.

20 - Climbing Like a Monkey

So, my mother tells me, "I will make it over, but I can't carry you or your hand or nothing."

And I said, "No! I am not going to!" because I know I cannot make it. Plus it's so cold, you touch the metal, your hands practically freeze to it, so your hands are not very limber; your hands are stiff and cold. The situation was so awful that I felt 100%, no doubt, that I cannot make it; I would fall. And when I think of one-meter jump, 'no'. I was not very athletic. I refused because I knew. You know sometimes when you know something about yourself, you know 'I can do it' or 'I cannot do it'—that is what goes. I cannot do that.

And even so, my mother was always very bossy, making me do things. She was asking me, "You think you can do it? If you think you can do it, you can do it."

And I said, "I know I cannot do it. I cannot."

At that point, my mother could see that this was not gonna happen. Not just because of me, because of the drama there altogether.

CHAPTER 21

THE RUSSIANS ARRIVE

People made it over the bridge to the middle part, and then they had no nerve to go on because the Russians were actually approaching, climbing over from the other side.

They push against the people with the machine gun, and they keep telling them, "Go! Go! Go! Go back! Go back!" Not physically shooting, but, like, 'if you don't go then we're gonna shoot.' And their commanding officers are yelling at them and screaming at them to keep going. Of course, they didn't speak German.

So now they push the people and they fall in the middle of the river and scream. And they fall by the tens and twenties together in groups, 'chu, chu, chu, chu, chu, chu, chu, chu,' people fall. Everybody looked gray and black in winter clothes they're wearing. It was horrible.

21- The Russians Arrive

That was going on when we decided we are turning around; we're leaving—we're going back. We don't know what we're going to face because in the meantime, the rest of the Russian army has proceeded and is already in the villages.

So, when we walk back from the bridge, we see some farmers left wagons, like the ladder-wagon, and bedding rolled together with the rope.

My mother, she says, "We can use all that."

The other lady had a baby carriage and had her baby in there. So we just start pulling the wagon. At first I walk with them, but I got distracted.

Suddenly, I can't find my mother. I got distracted because there was a lighthouse, and they have signals for the trains. Was nobody there anymore, but at that house there was a dog that I didn't really like because every time I walked there, he barked behind the chain-link fence and carries on. Now when I got by there, somebody had shot him. The dog was warm, still, lying down, dead. And so I spent a minute or two, I even opened up the chain-link fence and I went inside and I touched him.

I keep looking around, and there is this stone house where the train signalman used to live. The door was open and I walked in. There was a big room and there were all these Russian soldiers raping farm women that they picked out from all the people that, like us, were trying to go across and didn't make it. I don't know what they were doing! The women could see me because their face was up and the guy is on top of them.

The women start yelling, "Go away, child! Go away! Get out!"

"Okay, what did I do?" I don't know what they're doing at all.

So I finally got outside. My mother's standing where the trains used to go by, and back there I hear rifle shots, 'ch, ch, ch, ch, ch, ch, ch, ch,' a whole lot of shots. So I heard her yelling for me to come up there, and I make my way up there, but also at the same time all these machine gun fire.

My mother, she said, "They're shooting all those poor devils," but I don't know who they were.

I found out they were prisoners of war. The Germans came out of nowhere, bringing a whole army of prisoners of war in black and white striped suits. They wanted to take them away with them to do hard labor. And after the Americans were gone, and the Russians were coming, there is this moment of no enemy there—Russian or American. The Germans wanted to take that time to get these prisoners of war to some other location but they could see that was not possible, so they shot them all. And they fall down, and they were all lying there, dead, in the rain, on top of each other.

So we're walking with the wagon and it starts to rumble and rumble and a lot of the beddings that were tied together fall off the wagon and on top of the dead bodies.

My mother says, "Go get it! You climb down there and you get it and bring it back up here and put it on the wagon."

As I go climb there to get the bedding, I had to look at them, and they had their eyes open. I mean they were, "hoooo," and then they were shot so the eyes stayed open. And I try to find out 'are they alive or dead?' I had to walk on them, on the dead bodies, to get the damn featherbeds.

"Argh!" I was angry at my mother. I had to go and bring it... it's big, I'm not very big—I'm very skinny little thing. I carry it and pull it and bring it up. And she takes it from me and we put it on the little wagon. We keep walking, and another one falls down, altogether three times.

So then I refused, and I said, "I'm not going to go again."

Then when it happened again, she'd yell at me.

I said, "No." I was really mousy because my mother was such a devil.

The other woman, with the infant, she says, "Let her be! Just let's go!" So I was off the hook. We went and we left them behind.

So we walk and here comes some young Russian guy. He has a machine gun, and he shows that machine gun to my mother and he tips it like it's gonna shoot you if you don't come with me down in the forest. And I saw other women being pulled into the forest and screaming. So they did raping down there.

And I said, "What do they want to do, shoot those women?"

My mother said, "Yes." She didn't want to tell me; I didn't understand anyway.

The young Russian comes up and wants to get my mother to go in the woods with him—maybe was just seventeen, eighteen year old with blondish, medium-brown hair. He was so young and inexperienced and he wanted to, but he didn't really know how to tell her to come with him down there.

So, with her flirtative way, she holds him, and she says, "You speak English? Okay, you speak German?" I remember her saying that. And then she says, "Well, that's okay. You see my little children here? I'm bringing them to the village." She points to the village as she's saying these things in German—but he can see she's pointing to the village.

"We're going to the village, then I come back." I don't think he understood that.

He says, "Okay." So he didn't have the nerve to force her, like the others I saw pulling screaming women by the hair.

"Why do they scream, Mom? What are they doing?"

She says, "Never mind." She don't want to tell me; of course, I don't understand anyway.

So we keep going. We made it back to our village.

CHAPTER 22

CAPTURED BY THE RUSSIANS

There is a group of maybe ten or more, women of different ages, old German farmer-men they couldn't use in the war, and some children. And we're going onto the road that goes into the village. And so we just walk. It's such a small village—it has just five farms—so you can't go very far and you're out in the fields again.

They said, "What are we gonna do!?"

And my mother says to the others, "Never mind. We just go. We just walk." And so we just start walking real slow.

Our farm was the first one we crossed. Our farm lady had locked the gate which was built from wood so the hay wagons would fit in at harvest time. Our farm had walls like an old castle. Also, it had a small door for people to go in and out. All of it was locked.

22- Captured by the Russians

But the rest of the Russians had arrived, and they're sitting in front of our farm and they were sitting on top of their tanks.

The Russians say, "Ohhhhh! Frau, komm!" which means, "Woman, come!"

And my mother's smiling and trying to fool them. I know that she was trying to fool them. She's smiling and laughing, but we know it was a very serious situation. It's scary, but you don't cry.

"Let them think you like 'em," she said to us, "Let them think you like them very much, and smile at them."

Anyway, we walk by and had no idea where we were gonna go, except we're just gonna walk right now through this village.

At each farm they're sitting there, telling you, "Come on, open this gate!"

My mother would say, "It's not my farm. I don't know! I don't have a key!" Also, "We come back!" Ha, ha, ha, ha, ha. In German! We don't know who speaks German.

Little old farm women: they're short and they're fat, and they're wearing all these big crocheted blankets and shawls around them, and crying, crying—very scared.

And my mother says, "Shut up! Don't cry! Don't let them see you cry! Smile at them!"

Ha, ha, ha.

And I look, and I see we're approaching the last farm. And myself, too, my heart was just somewhere by my knees. It was the wealthiest farmer of the village; he had the biggest farm with lots of stables and a big gate. That gate was open, and a lot of Russians, on their tanks and trucks, were going in and out.

We approach and the little old ladies all said, "What are we gonna do?"

My mother said, "We're going in there like we own it, and we are going to just be nice, and we are going to smile at them."

We are not soldiers, we're not fighting them. They have obviously have taken over the place, but we know that we have to be nice to them because they have machine guns and we don't have nothing, and we don't know at all what's gonna happen.

Holding hands, the Russian soldiers had made a chain to block us from going any further and guide us to go into that farm. We walked in and and my mother insisted we smile, which was very scary to do because all these machine guns and the shots we had heard, and the people we had seen dying on the way. Not very easy. I was always just big-eyed. The only one who did good on the smiling was my mother.

So as we go into the farm, there's a big farmyard and all the stables and the houses where the farmers live. It's all-round, in a circle. It was all built in medieval days from stone and beams, like a fortress. In the middle is a pile of cow dung from the stables. That's the way they did it.

The Russians had it all worked out and they guide us to an open door and they shooed us all in a big room. Inside there's nothing, but two benches under two windows and in one corner a big, stone bowl. The big bowl is in this oven-like thing. There is a pump where you pump water in it. Underneath of it is a fire that keeps the water warm. This was a wash kitchen. The farmers used to put their laundry in there. They were pretty sophisticated for a medieval culture.

And right away my mother saw only two benches under the windows so she says, "All the children on the benches right now! Sit on it or lie down on it or go underneath and lie down."

The others follow in and all these people filled the room elbow to elbow. And it was still raining out there—wet, very cold and freezing—and getting dark slowly. We held onto each other to get warm.

And so my mother said, "You kids, lie down. Try to get some sleep."

The farm women were all whining, 'uheh, uheh, uheh.'

I was on the bench, peeking out the window and I see Russian soldiers out there, running back and forth.

My mother says, "Don't look. Don't let them see you; they'll shoot at you. Just sit there now or lie down on the bench or under the bench." And I remember having to go under the bench.

And then I wake up. It was night and dark. The kids were all lying down, but the older people were still standing there and whining. If you had to go to the bathroom, my mother directed the traffic.

"Make room in the middle for this person to go and pee in the drain, otherwise this was going to be all stinking in here." And that's what saved us before in the other place, too, with the Americans.

We were in there for ten days total like that.

22- Captured by the Russians

CHAPTER 23

JUMPING OVER THE RIVER FOR BREAD

The first morning, we had no food, nothing. But there was a water pump in the washroom, so we could get water. That is what they used for the washing, but it's clean water, really, because it's the country, and you can drink it.

So we're just all in there and we don't know what is next. We have to be afraid of the Russians because they had a reputation, wow! They kill people. They rape people. We have seen that, but I didn't understand that it was raping and what that was. So we're lucky enough to have a hole to pee in and that we have water to drink.

Often, when I couldn't sleep, I'd make my way on the bench and look out the window at what the Russians are doing out there. They're carrying on and get so drunk! And they play accordions; balalaikas, a triangle, guitar-like looking thing; and they sing. Wow. I loved the Russian music, the very "boom!" strong!

He, he, he, he, he, he, ha.

So, my mother comes up with this idea. She said, "Okay. They are known to actually like children. So we don't know, but we're gonna have to do something." So my mother said, "Well it's still the war, and they're not gonna let us out, but whenever they look at you, you smile at them—no matter what you think." So she was telling everybody that.

They hear her but still whine.

And then, she hears the metal wagon being brought in. I heard it, too. It looked to me like an engine of a train, by itself. It was not quite as strong and thick like an engine is, but that shape: round, black, chimney on it, and all of that. And they drive it in through the yard. They put it next to the barns. And they start making fire in there, and you can see the fire and the smoke. Then they start baking bread.

And my mother says "Aha! Baking bread. We're gonna have food."

Nobody else believed that. When we smelled the bread, there was no holding back.

So now, she arranged something. They had two Russian soldier guards outside the door of this washroom. They were instructed not to let us out at all, and if we tried to go, shoot. And they had the machine gun.

So she said, "They don't look too mean." So my mother said, "Okay, let the children through! Line 'em up. Now you line up. I'm gonna open the door." The Russians don't see us— they're out there. "Now walk out the door here, and you go one after the other."

The farm woman said, "No, no, no!"

And my mother says, "They're not gonna kill 'em. They're not gonna kill the kids! You go out, and you walk all in a circle around that pile of cow dung, passing by where the bread is being baked."

In the yard, the pee of the cows coming out of the stables collects and it makes a river. It's almost black as it goes through, and out into the garden. That's how the farmers used to fertilize their gardens.

"And then when you come to the river, you jump over it. And because you're jumping over, they're gonna reward you and give you bread. Then you keep walking, and when you come back here to the front door of the washroom, I'll be standing there with the Russians and you give me the bread."

Everybody thought she's nuts. But you know what, she was right. And I hoped, I prayed in my mind. I thought, 'cow dung can't kill me if I fall in. It's not deep, it's just, well, you're gonna be stinking to the high heaven. But who cares, we probably stunk anyway.' I thought, 'I know they're gonna be surprised and they're gonna probably think it's funny.'

So we go around in a circle, and when we come to the river, we jump. A river is too much of a word; it's just like a creek of pee.

So, when we come there, my mother said, "Put your legs together and jump over, and when you make it, they will reward you by giving you some bread."

Everybody jumped it—except my little brother. He's just barely over two years old. He had long pants on, and little shoes and a coat. He's the last one because he's so short and so little and he can't run fast as we did.

'Crk, crk, crk,' we jump and then we keep going.

The Russians, they thought that was so funny, "Ah! Ha, ha, ha!" They love children.

Here comes my brother, and then he stops right there on the edge of the creek of pee and he jumps right in the middle!

Ha, ha, ha!

And he's to his knees full of poo-poo. And they laugh, laugh, laugh. And he laughs, too. And we run around again.

My mother meets us, standing between the two Russians right there at the gate. She takes the bread and gives it to the people behind her.

She said, "Divide it fairly and keep some for the children." She said, "Go again!"

So we're going again, and as we pass the wagon where the bread was being baked—there were several of them working it—they gave my brother the bread. And he's the last one coming.

So my mother said, "Come up here, come here!" to come there because the two Russians with the machine guns was not gonna let my mother go out.

So we go again. We had about three-bread, minimum, from one run-around. My brother, he's the one. He was feeding all these people

Ha, ha, ha!

They were very conscious about it, breaking fresh bread between all the people.

The next day when they fired it back up, "Ah, yes. They're doing it again," my mother would say.

That went on for a few days, but now comes the end of the war.

23- Jumping Over the River for Bread

CHAPTER 24

COMRADES IN VICTORY

The day of the end of the war: During the night, as we all sleep, the Russians are out there every night making music. But it was extra loud and they were shooting rockets into the air. They had little rockets that "choo!" go up. It was extra loud and the sky was red with all those rockets and all that going on.

All the old people were crying out loud, "They're gonna kill us all now!"

My mother said, "Shut up! The war is over! Don't you see that? They're celebrating the war is over and they won! We're gonna open the door, and you grab 'em and you kiss 'em! Russians kiss right and left. Go there and you do that and you go, 'Oh, comrade, comrade!' that's their word for friend. And you do that, and you sit with them by the fire. You just act like you're not afraid of them because they are your saviors. They're the one who saved your life."

So my mother was preaching—"War is over"

And they were still, "Wah, wuh, wuh, wuh, woo, woo, woo." —whining.

And so she kicked the door open and the two soldiers just let her go! They did not stop anybody! So we're all out. Then she made us kids go back in to go lie down and sleep. She didn't trust them too much. And we don't want to drink vodka anyway.

I remember watching an old man who had cried.

My mother had yelled at him, "Don't you let them see you cry! You smile and kiss 'em! Kiss 'em! Kiss 'em!"

Ha, ha, ha, ha!

The Russians were already wiped out from their vodka. And two of them take the old man, right and left, hit him on the shoulder,

"Yay! Comrade!"

And he starts smiling. He didn't know what was happening. They make little bonfires out there. Around the bonfire, they drink, and they make music, and they sing. That was something they do every night anyway, but this time they celebrated the winning of the war.

They went all night long and you could see people getting tired. They fall down here and there. They start sleeping behind the barn doors in the yard.

But she said, "When the sun comes up, get up and go back to your farm!"

So we did, and so did the others. Suddenly, everybody was gone. Everybody went back to their farm they usually lived on and celebrated with the Russians to keep them happy. And this is when my mother and that woman were checking out the next door farm and found the damn horse.

Ha, ha, ha, ha, ha!

24- Comrades in Victory

CHAPTER 25

ESCAPE ON A PAINTED HORSE

In the morning, my mother said, "Okay, get your stuff and get out. Everybody go back where you stayed."

So, my mother and that other woman that had the infant, we're going back to the same farm. At our farm, the Russians were partying too.

Ah, ha, ha.

The next farm down had a lot of prisoners of war all this time; I don't know how long—months or years. One of them, she got totally blasted. This was all in this early morning hours; it was still foggy and half-dark outside. She got all crazy. She went inside to the farmer's bedroom, and she put on whatever she found. She had scarves. All her hair, it was all waves from the braids.

I stood at the door, watched her, "wow!"

She didn't see me at all. She was happy, dancing and singing loudly in her language. A man, a prisoner of war from her country grabbed her and took her out of there. And I saw her run into the street. I hear the Russians coming, with Jeeps and other vehicles—she jumps right on top of the hood, and she sings to them.

Some of these Yugoslavian men were embarrassed. She was from their country and they found it embarrassing. And then they go up there and they grab her down and tell her to get in the house. And she did but, kept singing.

Then, my mother came and told me to get out of there. My mother, in the meantime, had been talking to the other woman who had this little infant. And they told me, "Stay here with the baby. We're just gonna go check out the farm across on the other side."

That farm was deserted; the farmers had left a long time ago. Then the Americans had taken it over and made it a communication station. But they were gone, and they had left some equipment there that didn't work, and there was a horse. A lonely, lonely horse stood there with a wagon attached to it. And it had blinders on his eyes and it looked very tired. It just kept standing there, picking up one foot to rest and then after a while another one to rest. And it just stood there, like 'I don't care.' It was gray, kind of fog-gray, with little dark spots, sort of Appaloosa-type horse. It was dirty, and filthy, and spotted silver-gray, but even so, it was too white still.

My mother and that lady with the baby chased all over that farm, looking to find some black paint. They say, "We have to paint that horse black because we're gonna walk with that horse to escape."

When the first light comes up, we want to make it down to Güterglück, which is the little town five kilometers from there where the trains start and end. My mother had heard from somebody, somewhere, that there is a train that's standing there. It has been standing there for about two weeks or something, but now it is going to leave at 2:15 a.m. and go to Berlin. So we don't care what kind of train it is, as long as it rolls.

And so, they were looking for some black paint, dark color, anything dark. On that farm, they finally found a half a can full of tar, black tar and smeared it on the horse. And that horse just stood there, and they painted it as good as they could. Now, not very good, but, you know, just make him filthy.

Ha, ha, ha, ha, ha, ha.

The poor horse just stood there.

And then, they got us out of the farmhouse, loaded the bedding and bundles of clothes. The lady with the baby had to leave the baby carriage; it was too big for this two-wheel coach. So she had to hold her baby with blankets.

And this is all cobblestone pavement, so the wheels go, 'cr, cr, cr.' My mother and the lady, they also found a bunch of burlap sacks and they had stripped them and they had wrapped them all around the wheels and tied it with rope. The wooden wheels had a rim of metal and it made it a little softer—so we did not make much noise. So we took off.

My mother, "They don't even hear us. I think they're all drunk. This is good for us."

Because we couldn't trust anybody. We didn't trust the Russians; we don't know what they're gonna do. Right there the Russians were not bad to us, but their reputation was very bad and scary.

Anyway, we made the five kilometers like that, with that horse, just going very slow, one step, 'nother step, 'nother.

Ha, ha, ha, ha, ha.

It had all his tack on.

Two Berlin ladies, what do they know?

Ha, ha, ha.

And then, when we got there, and we saw the train, we stop. We all got off, take the stuff off—the luggage, and bye to the horse, and we went over to the trains.

Now we started to open the wagons, and they were not passenger cars—they were freight cars, and they had the big doors that slide.

Then Mother said to the lady—I heard her, "I think this is the trains that they used to bring the people to the concentration camps."

We want to get on that train if it leaves for Berlin, so that's all that counted. But it's too hard for them to open the sliding doors; they're very heavy.

Finally, they opened one and then they go, "Oh no! It's filthy."

It was poo on the floor. People must have been in here a while and they had to go wherever. And it was all in the mounds all around the wagons. And so we went in the one had the least of it, which was still a lot. We had to find spots where we could hold onto the wall and not be right in the poop. The wagons had no furnishings, no seats, no nothing—just plain open space.

We waited, and my mother was watching on a watch: 2:15, 'clew, clack,' the train starts moving. When a train like that starts, the wagons hit together and then they pull apart as they get going. You have to hold yourself upright.

25- Escape on a Painted Horse

And when it started to move she says, "2:15 with German punctuality!"

I, ha, remember exactly how she would say that, ha, ha. And they were laughing, happy it moved, no matter what the conditions. And then it started to speed up quite a lot and it did not stop anywhere else. And it made the way straight through.

It was a two-and-a-half-hour trip to Berlin from Flötz. And when it drove into Berlin, it drove into the main train station, called Hauptbahnhof, which means "main train station," which had suffered under the bombing. And all the big glass domes that were over it were broken; it was just the metal frames. I remember looking at that because I had always seen it before in its glory. But the platforms were there and the trains were coming in and stopping. People were coming in and out, wherever they all came from.

So, my mother and the lady pushed those heavy doors open, and they look if there's anybody to help us out. The platform's built for people, so it's actually a high step.

But no, no. People were busy. Everybody had expressions of being, '[gasp],' fanatic, just, 'get, get, get going.' Women, man, any old and young, everybody came with some other train, got off, and wanted to get out.

There is a chance normally to transfer to other lines. Berlin is a very large city, it's like a little country on its own. Anyway, we know where we would want to go normally, so we get into the S-Bahn, the electric trolley.

We got on and they're city folks—they are rush rush rush, go go go. Nobody looks at you; nobody sees that you're filthy, and that you have torn shoes, and that your hair hasn't been combed. Nobody looks at each other. Everybody is anxious to get on the right train and get out of there. Everybody had a very anxious expression. All these round eyes, like chickens that are scared to get butchered.

That was our first step back in Berlin.

25- Escape on a Painted Horse

CHAPTER 26

MAKING FLAGS OVERNIGHT

We made it to Tempelhof and we were lucky that our apartment was still there and standing. There was not a splinter of glass that was not already pulverized. No windows at all. All the doors were out and the walls between were down. What a sight! But it was there, so never mind that, we would fix it. And I would complain,

"Where's my this? Where's my that?"

Ha, ha, ha.

My mother would tell me to hush up.

Ha, ha, ha, ha, ha.

"You have the place, that's what counts!"

And so, adults got together and they collected nails and they collected anything to cover your windows. Not with glass, because there wasn't any, but, you know, with cardboard or wooden planks or anything you could find.

And we, the children, had to go out and look for little wood pieces and all that could be used for heating in the tile ovens, which we had in the rooms. We also look for candles and other things that would make a little light because we had no light; there was no electricity, of course. It was cold, too, of course, always blowing through.

The bathroom and the kitchen had pipes for water, but they were broken, and then there was zero water at all for a long, long time. So, just imagine you have no water, can't wash your hands, can't brush your teeth.

There was nothing to buy and you wanted food. All you ever wanted is food, so you go in the ruins and whatever you found that is still good, maybe somebody wants to exchange that for food. So the black market was where the people get some food, some kind of meat. Rabbit is common to be eaten in Europe, but they had no head, they had no paws, they had no tail, how do we know it's a rabbit?

My mother would say, "It is the neighbor's old little fat dachshund!"

Ha, ha, ha, ha.

Then she also would look out the window and see people walk, and she say, "The ladies always used to walk with little dogs. Have you noticed there are no more dogs?"

Ah, ha, ha, ha, ha.

She was always making fun of it; it was sad, but you had to keep your humor going not to crack up. Because a lot of people did crack up. So, in any case, that was the daily life, and this is before the blockade.

So now, these four: the Amis, as we called the Americans; and the Russians, the Ruskies, and the English were the Bobbies; and the French, Michaël. To us, they were all warriors, and nobody liked any of them, of course. Not the Germans either! I mean, they were glad that they lost the war. People were afraid of the Russians; some had many Russian stories. All these stories were around you, you heard people talk about these things.

Nobody was celebrating because you have to look for where you're gonna sleep tonight, and what you're gonna eat. And we just wanted to find our stuff and see how we can live. And where's your kid, and where's your mother, and where's your husband? Everybody was lost.

The American, the Russian, the British, and the French armies came and took Germany together.

26- Making Flags Overnight

The Russians had the entire part of Germany around Berlin, which included Berlin. Berlin is the capital, and it's bigger than any town or city in Germany, and so they all wanted it. It was, however, in the Russian sector. The Americans and the others are objecting that the Russians claim all of Berlin.

They say, "We've divided the country into the four sectors, but we cannot also divide that city because it is the capital."

That kind of talk went on and on. It was posted in the newspapers on a round barrel in the street, called Litfaßsäule. The newspaper people used to glue the newspaper pages open onto that barrel because they didn't had enough money to print papers for everybody, so it was posted. And people stood there, reading.

So now, each district of Berlin became the ownership of another country. And we had no money. All the money, even all the coins had Hitler's picture on it—that was the currency.

But, the Russians say, "Don't bring this money to anybody; it's no good."

None of them want to accept it, but you could exchange some of your money into new money. They made some emergency money, printed only on one side, but it didn't last long. It was changing and changing and changing, almost overnight—the next day, "You can throw all that money away, we have a new one."

And so it went continuously like that for a while.

They said, "Okay, this part of Berlin, Tempelhof," where we were, and Schöneberg next door, "this is the Russian sector. So, by tomorrow, you have to have a red flag."

That lets them know that you are Communist. So everybody had one, except us; my mother would not allow it. I was questioned by other children about it when we played in the street.

One little boy says to me, "Everybody has red flag out; how come you don't have one?"

I told my mother that's what they ask me.

She says, "You tell them we're still making it. We're making a flag."

"Oh, okay."

So I told the kids that and they say, "Oh, okay."

She didn't believe in flags because we had too much trouble with all of this Hitler stuff and the flags. If you don't have one and they come to your house and they knock on the door,

"How come you don't have a flag out?"

26- Making Flags Overnight

People got arrested. Everybody has the flag out, not just on Hitler's birthday or whatever reasons. I remember I was looking at a field of flags out the windows. You couldn't hardly see the windows because it was flags waving all the time.

Now, we're supposed to have a red flag overnight, but they didn't had red flags, so they take the old Hitler flag and took off the white swastika circle in the middle. It was just like a patch sewn on, and then it's all red. Everybody put out the red Communist flag.

And I'm playing outside on the sidewalk with some friends and we see this man. And he goes out and he hangs a red flag. And I can see that the red circle in the middle is very dark red and the rest of it is kind of bleached out from the sun because it used to be the Hitler flag.

Ha, ha, ha.

And I said, "Oh! I know what that was!"

He just looked at me and he took it down and he closed his door. And later I saw he had it put back out. So he was afraid he's gonna be declared a Nazi or something.

So, okay. Our featherbeds that everybody has, has a red lining, so everybody took them out and made a flag overnight. But it's just plain red and you didn't had to do anything much just attach it to some broomstick and hang it out your window. Red flag, we're Communists: we are okay. Don't shoot up here.

Ha, ha, ha, ha.

But then they changed the mind. Maybe two days later, the story is, "Uh, uh. No, no. No. We are American sector."

My mother said, "What in the world? How you make an American flag?" They hardly knew what it looked like.

Overnight, my mother got everybody in our building in our one-room; we could heat this one small room and it will be warm.

"So, all your kids, bring a blanket, bring a pillow and you lie down."

There was no electricity, so everybody looked for leftover candles from Christmas and stuff to have a little lamp. And they would not make big light. Mother called them funzels.

Ha, ha, ha. A funzel! It's just like a little glow.

So they're sitting around with that little light, and they're trying to sew a flag. They take a featherbed apart, cut it. You have to have the feathers flying out the window and make a mess, but doesn't matter: we need the piece of red material. And

26- Making Flags Overnight

then, they strip white sheets and now we sew those by hand onto the red.

They say, "How many stripes?"

My mother would say, "Who cares? Just put 'em on there, as many as it fits. Don't make 'em too small!" Some of them had all these small and some had big.

So, ha. Ha ha ha.

So we need at least two, three flags to hang out the windows on different floors. It's to let them see, "Hey, we're here. We're for the Americans; don't shoot at us." You know, that's all we worried about—them shooting at us—because they were always shooting at us.

Also, we have to have that blue rectangle on the flag; nobody had blue material just like that, nobody.

She said, "Okay, everybody look at home if you have ink," because people were still writing with the ink and the feather for nice letters. "So, now everybody look in the household if you find any drip of ink, bring it here and we'll dye some white material blue." And they actually managed to get enough ink.

Somebody else cut white stars out another piece of sheet to put on there after.

And they would say to my mother, "How many?"

"I don't know! Nobody knows!" My mother saying, "Just make a bunch of stars!"

So they did, as many as fit. And then they had tried to make glue out of some flour they found with water, and then they had tried to sew them on with yarn, which was very tedious work because we only had one night. It got so heavy after all the layers, like a quilt, that it wouldn't blow in the wind.

So, my mother said, "Let's nail the flag to kitchen window board, and then let it hang down the building." Of course, we had no glass in the windows anyway.

The Americans probably didn't realize how paranoid the German people were about this flag thing because under Hitler you could get arrested and taken away if you didn't put a flag out. So it was a very scary idea. And now these aliens that we don't even know come from another part of the world and they're telling us what flag to hang. So, we obeyed, just to have peace and quiet and save our lives.

And that's how we got an American flag. And that is the beginning of the American sector in Berlin.

26- Making Flags Overnight

CHAPTER 27

CHIPMUNKING

There was a blockade for five years. The Russians got very mad and they said, "No. We are not allowing any food being brought in through this part of Berlin that you call West—American, French, or British. We have the Communist part—we will bring food there—but the rest of Berlin, the three other sectors, will not be allowed to bring any food in. And you cannot go through—in or out." Nothing; everything blockaded. Five years!

They started to give out some coupons for rationing of food—long lines for that. So my daily activity was standing in line. So this was the life.

There was nothing that did not need to be repaired. Street lights, holes in the ground, and the houses. You had to do it somehow. People voluntarily, women mostly, go on the street outside the houses and bring a chair and a hammer. They collect all the bricks from the broken-down houses that had been bombarded. They hammer off the mortar so it's clean. They make nice rectangular mountains of them, and then another one and another.

And people say, "There will be a day when they rebuild things and they will need those bricks. We can't do it now, but we can clean 'em off and have 'em ready."

And that was all over that huge city of Berlin, every street. They called them the Ruin Women and built a statue memorial for that in Berlin.

Thousands of people live there, and we have to try to eat. So anybody who had flower boxes—flowers go out, 'crk.' We put the sand in and we put something that will be eatable, like maybe we have some seeds or something.

Our apartment building was like a big square, with four different streets bordering it, and in the middle was all grass and a trash-house. We all divided it, divided it by so many units of apartments. You get a little wooden stick and then put a little bit of cord and make like a fence which is the division. And if you find a way, you can grow things there to eat. There were ways of buying seeds on the black market, exchanging for your silver, for your jewelry, for anything valuable.

One person in my apartment building had two or three rabbit cages on his balcony—we called Kaninchen, the kind that you domesticate. And then he had two or three chickens in the basement. They could go out the little window that is even with the ground there and scratch. And they lay some eggs, and then once a while, he sacrificed a chicken. And he also butchered his rabbits. This is how people helped themselves.

We would go and do hamstern, which, translated, means, "chipmunking." We go and we try to find food. We started to go to the woods. First, we looked through all the old books, any books that were medical books. People in the 1800's, they had books that show you all the herbs that grow in the wild, and what they're good for, and how you should harvest them. Also about the mushrooms that grow in the wild. When you're a big-city person, you don't really look into that, but now they all did look into it.

We were looking up where berries, like blueberries and boysenberries grow. And a lot of people didn't had the right information and a lot of people died of poison mushrooms, were getting the wrong mushroom.

I see people have baskets full of mushrooms that they collected. I knew they were poisonous because I had been studying the books. So I was saying to some young boys, like fourteen, fifteen-year-olds, who're sitting there watching over some baskets,

I said, "These are poisonous."

And they go, "Get away, you stupid!" throwing lumps of dirt at me and stuff. So, I just didn't do that anymore. And it's not that I was any smarter, I just had access to these kind of books.

And the children, we have to climb into these broken-down, ruined houses and see if there's anything in the basements; we find books. But children want to play hide-and-seek. We play catch and all of that. We just, you know, do what children do. When you're a kid you don't care.

And then we learned a lot about the herbs on the side of the railroad tracks. And they bloom certain seasons for each and everything. And we learned to pick big, yellow blooms that come up in the fall, called the Emperor's Candles. And they grow wild, as a weed. So we kids have to jump on the railroad tracks and pick them. It was dangerous.

There was another weed called the Burning Nettle. They have edges like a chainsaw. And they have fine, little hair all over the green leaf, and if you touch it, it burns like crazy, and that's why it got the name the Burning Nettle.

So, my mother made thick, thick mittens out of military blankets—that the soldiers drop here and there, several layers on top each other and then sew 'em together by hand. We have to wear them to pick the Burning Nettle and put 'em in a rucksack, backpacks.

At home, once the water is boiling, boiling, boiling, making bubbles, you put the nettles in there. Right away, they collapse and they no longer burn, and they make a wonderful spinach. Tasted real good. And so we pick a lot of things from the woods. Berlin has a lot of woods, lakes, and rivers going through. To get there was another thing because it was hard to get to these places, but we did, somehow.

So, we tried to sneak at night, and they took all the kids along, and we all were trained not to make a sound. We're going to the outskirts of Berlin, out of Berlin: now we are in Russian zone. There are farms, like fruit plantations.

My mother knew one plantation owner because his daughter was a ballet dancer, too. And we had gone there before the war and visited. The kids had a good time picking berries. And he had a big press in his basement and he was making cranberry juice and everything out of the fruits. He also grew peaches, apples, plums—the blue ones—, and cherries, too. Oh my God, kids, we loved cherries.

So, we're picking, picking, picking fruits, however he gives us, in exchange, a lot of baskets

27- Chipmunking

of fruit. Now, we have to sneak back to the border at night, in the dark, to get back into West Berlin.

As we go through, "Hi! Ha, ha, ha!" All the kids sitting on top of this secret compartment in this car. However, we got caught with the fruits.

Russian soldiers found it. They weren't that stupid; they already know. They said, "No, where you have it? Where you have it?"

We say, "We don't have nothing!"

And they wouldn't believe it. And they have already found out how many tricks people use, and so they took all the baskets of cherries. It was really heart wrenching.

And my mother and some of the women—these were all women—said to them, "How can you do that? These children are starving!"

And so we took some and put them in our ears and things—kids, you know. They made us take them off our ears and where we had 'em hung on buttons and stuff, and throw 'em into a dumpster-type thing. They would not even let us have that.

And then they were threatening us and said, "If we will catch you again, we will put you in forced-labor."

So we go back empty-handed into starving West Berlin. So that was the blockade.

CHAPTER 28

ALL GREEN

I was very skinny, not having much heat in my body to hold up. I would get very sick all the time. I started running big fevers and I fainted all the time. I was proud of showing off my ribs to my friends, "Now, in another week, the last two will come out!"

When you're a kid, you don't see any tragedy.

So, in the meantime, my mother heard from some source that there was an organization that wanted to help. The Americans made what they called "The Program." The children were sent, with the American military to free-willing, volunteer foster parents in West Germany, which was not blockaded. And the people already started to get better there. They had food; they could go to store and actually buy food.

My mother went to this source and said, "I have two children and I would like to have them go to foster care."

And they said, "We don't have any more foster volunteers. However, if you know somebody that you can write to in West Germany, ask them, we bring 'em there to West Germany. However, we cannot help with any money or anything else, and we cannot guarantee how long this will be because we don't know when the blockade will end, if at all."

My mother found an address and name. She used to be a dancer, too, in the ballet. I don't know how the heck she found her 'cause she wasn't even in touch with that lady anymore. This is before computers, you know. It's quite remarkable; I have no idea how, but she did get in touch with her.

And she answered back. And she said yes, she's married, and she knows that the foster child could be a long time. So that's what she needs to tell her husband, and she did.

He said, "Okay."

Finally, my mother finally got word. So the Americans looked at me. I had all these ribs to show and they enrolled me. They said my brother's not skinny enough—still baby fat on his cheeks.

They said, "Okay, she can go to West Germany with these people that said yes."

So I was sent, and it was my very first flight I ever had. I had to be brought by my mother to the airport where they had collected all these children, and then they loaded the planes.

The plane had just come over with a load of coal and things they brought in from West Germany to be distributed to West Berliners. So it had the aluminum floors inside with coal dust all over. There were no seats inside that plane. However, there were these military canvas straps attached to the wall that go underneath your leg; and then you all sit along the wall with your back to the windows. The plane was full, maybe fifty, sixty kids. So we sit down, and somehow they tied us on.

And then the plane took off. And everybody on board got so sick, except me. I was very sick, too, but I didn't throw up. They all threw up, so the floor was ew, and I felt so sick I want to die.

I pray inside, "Please let me throw up!"

I felt if I could throw up, maybe I'll feel better. But I don't want to fall into all that throw-up and coal dust. It was terrible.

It was a two-hour flight. When they landed, I must have looked really awful. They opened the doors. They didn't put stairs up like you used to see on airplanes. American military trucks and American soldiers come stepping up to the door,

28- All Green

and we now line up one by one up to this door—first the really little ones, so sick, aw I remember them—then an American soldier will pick you up, and give you to another soldier and he put you on this truck.

So when I came up, the soldier looked at me. He said two English words, "All green!" because I looked all green from being sick.

Anyway, they picked me up, too. I was so skinny, so little. I was maybe taller than some of the little three-year-olds that came before me, but I was lighter. But I was glad to have been out of that plane.

We go in the trucks and they were loaded with nuns. I remember looking at the nuns with the robes. I was not really familiar with this kind of people.

The trucks start moving and they said to us, "We're going to a hospital, and in that hospital, you will be able to clean up. You will have a nice, warm bed, and you will get food."

That word went around in seconds. All the little kids, everybody understood "food." I didn't care about cleaning up or bed, nothing. Food, yes.

So we're driving out of the airport and into the streets. I think it was Nuremberg. We go through the streets: bombed buildings and all was an everyday sight, we're used to that. Then we see stores! Grocery stores, at this time in Germany, would have fresh produce on the streets, right in front of the store. They would have these wooden boxes full of pears, full of apples, and above will be big bunches of bananas hanging down. Never any of us ever seen a banana.

We go "Ohhh!"

And I heard the other kids to the front get off the seat, "What is that? What is that?"

And then some nuns say, "This is oranges, or this is bananas." The word shot through the whole truck. Everybody heard the word "bananas".

"Where? Where? What? Can we have some?"

"Yes, after we get where you're going." And the nuns had tears—crying.

We didn't understand.

So when we get to the hospital, it was one room, lower floor and the doors are all open and there's nice, clean sheets, and we're so filthy.

Another lady comes with a cart and they say, "Put the clothes in here. We're washing it. You get it back clean tomorrow. In the meantime, you wear this shirt. And stay on your bed because a dinner cart is gonna come through."

Running back to the bed, very excited, and sitting there, waiting.

28- All Green

The nurses come through with the carts and have the hot food, and they spooned it right out on the plates. Ahh, I was in the bed close to the corridors, seeing it right there.

And then one girl says, "They have meat!"

And everybody went, "Meat! Meat!"

We heard the word, and know what it is, but we did not had meat for a long time.

So, I jump out of the bed and run up to the hot cart, "Show me the meat! Just want to see! Wow! This is meat!"

And then we get the plate.

"Can we have more?"

And they said, "No, we only have this much, it's all measured out for all the kids here, but tomorrow morning we bring you breakfast."

So we look outside the window; volunteers had hung balloons all outside our windows. So we don't need to go nowhere; we love it here. There was the food, there were balloons outside—who needs to go somewhere else?

And they laugh and they say, "Don't worry, you're going to have nice foster parents, and you're going to have good food every day." Say all these nice things.

'Can I trust that? I'm already here; this is good.'

Just like they said, in the morning, they brought us breakfast, they gave us our clean clothes. And I start feeling sad that I have to leave because now I realize kids most likely, don't go on the same train because one goes here, one goes there. Even you met the children only the day before, at the airport, they're somebody who understand because we lived the same thing. And so that was kind of hard, too.

28- All Green

CHAPTER 29

POTATO SHOES

My foster home was in a village outside of Kassel, called Waldau. I had a little backpack my mother had made from a military blanket—we used for hamstern, too. In it, I had my little dolls that I treasured from my home.

My foster parents say, "Okay, take everything out and put it here so we see what you got."

I bring out my dolls, "This is Hannelore, and this is so and so."

"Uhmm. What else?"

"No, that's all."

And they said, "You don't have any clothes?"

"No... I don't think we had any..." Because we had very little.

So they go, "Oh, wow."

And I had no toothbrush and they got mad about that. I say, "Well, there was. Yeah, I had one. Oh. We didn't pack it. I guess we forgot it."

The man said, "I cannot afford to buy a toothbrush." The man would not get me a toothbrush, which, I found out, was seventy-five cents.

And there was another problem: I didn't had shampoo—they didn't had shampoo—and I couldn't wash my hair, which became a big problem. I got dandruff, and the teachers in school found out and sent me to the principal.

And they look and they found out and say, "Who watches over you?"

"Oh, my Tante Ellen, but she can't buy any because her husband does not allow that—too much money."

And I remember that principal said, "Really?"

"Yes. He doesn't allow it."

So they wrote a letter to my Auntie Ellen.

"Now you take that with you and you give it to her, not him." They asked her to come to the school and talk to the principal.

And the next day, she came to school at a certain time they gave her. I had to sit outside the door as they had Auntie Ellen in there. When the door opened and teachers go through, I see them checking her hair and asking her things.

Two days later, the teacher brought a box and it had about four little mini bottles of shampoo from the U.S. Army.

And they said, "This is for you to use and do not let Auntie Ellen use it. Her husband has to buy her shampoo."

Tante Ellen would never say something against him because she knows which side her bread is buttered, as my mother called it. If he puts her out she had nothing.

Then, I didn't had no clothes, so she put out the word to neighbors, "We have this child and she has no clothes."

In a little village, everybody knows each other and any little gossip goes around like wildfire. So all the neighbors came together and brought clothes out of their closets that they no longer wanted, no matter what size. And together they made patterns, and they made clothes. They made me nice coats and dresses, also knitting gloves and socks. I got everything.

A volunteer man used the canvas bags and satchels soldiers throw away, and made the top of shoes. A wooden sole had upholstery nails all around, holding the canvas to the wooden soles. I didn't had any other shoes than that.

And the principal in the school, he says, "What are these potatoes doing on your feet?"

I said, "That's my shoes!"

And he says, "Well who made that?"

I told him, and the principal arranged that I get shoes. He wrote out some paper, it said, "This child needs shoes." Sent one to my auntie, and one to the American army.

So, then we got word back. They said we got to come now to Kassel, and there at the American barracks, they have all kind of donated, second-hand shoes from America they brought over. They were kind of tough, get-blister material, but in any case, I put them on, and the Americans wanted to keep the old potato ones.

They said, "Can we have it?"

I think they wanted to show off how some of these kids walk around. They took 'em and they laugh.

Then, we walk back to the truck where the man was sitting out there, waiting. And he would have nothing nice to say. All through the trip, he would say "You and your American friends, your Amis."

I don't know what he was saying. The man was brainwashed from Hitler, still, or something. Who knows? So that was this thing with him.

Then, somewhere, somehow, a fire broke out at the school building. I mean, whoo, big. So we're all out, out, out, and we stay around outside and then the fire department comes. It was very poor—everything was destroyed from the war. They didn't had much of fire department hoses or anything—so I watched my school burn to the ground.

I remember an old man standing next to me as all the people watch the building burning. The top floor collapsed into the next floor, 'foo,' and then more flames, and then the next one.

The old man next to me said, "Oh, you're so lucky. All the years I went to school, they were so strict; they'd spank us with a stick. I prayed my school building would burn down and it never did."

Ha ha ha ha ha ha ha, ha.

So anyway, I was happy, too, that the school actually burned down. But it was a big loss and we didn't had a school building anymore. The building is down—we can't go inside. But they insisted we go to school. There was a fountain in the middle of the schoolyard, but now it was just a round circle of stone. So we would all sit in a circle and the teacher walks around it and talks to the kids.

Finally, Auntie Ellen said, "Look, tell this teacher you cannot come and sit out there in the cold with the rain coming down, sick all the time."

So that was the end of that teacher teaching us and all of that.

CHAPTER 30

HERR TÜCHLER RETURNS

Back in Berlin, I was outside our apartment with other kids, playing hopscotch. From all the broken houses, there was the inside drywall, broken in pieces all over the streets. And we use it as a chalk for whatever which is mostly hopscotch.

Ha, ha, ha. Kids find a way.

Anyway, we were playing hopscotch on the sidewalk. It was not snow; it must have been spring. Here comes this man with a nice suit, with his fedora, and a little briefcase.

And he looks, and he says, "Ingrid?"

And I say, "Oh! Herr Tüchler!"

Oh, we just jumped him and we hug him and we laugh. "You came back!"

He says, "Yes."

I said, "Where have you been so long?"

He says, "In China."

I said, "Ha, ha, ha! How did you get to China? How in the world did you get to China? It's a long way."

"I know," he says.

He says, "Well, the underground."

And I kept thinking an underground train, but it isn't. It was an organization of the Jewish people and sympathizers who got together to create ways to get Jews secretly out of the country and shipped to other countries. And he got there with his sister.

And I say, "Where's his sister?"

"Ah," he says, "she loved China, but she got very sick and died in China."

"Oh," I said, "really?"

"Yeah. It's best that way," he said.

And then I said, "So you're here? Why come back here?"

And he says, "Look, this is home."

How can he think he's at home? The people have been put to death—his people and everybody else—because of the war. How hard it must have been on those people that survived. But he felt it was home, and he had to be back.

Isn't that amazing, how connected some people are to home?

He lived there and everything in the apartment was the way he left it, except all the glass. Nobody had glass windows—are you kidding? They had shattered early on.

So he didn't had anything to mourn about except for his sister. He was happy; he smiled. He was like his quiet self. But he wanted to come home to die. This was his home.

I never got over that.

THE END

THANK YOU
WE HOPE YOU ENJOYED
RED SKY NIGHTS

audio, digital and print editions available

www.echoludo.com

RED SKY NIGHTS

www.ingramcontent.com/pod-product-compliance
Lightning Source LLC
Chambersburg PA
CBHW052033070526
44584CB00016B/2017